TWO FOR JOY

JUST A FEW WORDS ON BIRDS

Jean Hendy-Harris

Chalk Pits Press

Copyright Jean Hendy-Harris 2020

Other titles

Chalk Pits Press
Chalk Pits and Cherry Stones
Eight Ten to Charing Cross
In Disgrace with Fortune
More than Just Skeletons
Sunday's Child
Deceived by Faith

Putting The Joy Back Into Egypt (Hodder & Stoughton)
Creative Pathways (I & II) (Ashton Scholastic)

Contents

A Cage Fit for Eagles 1
The Pigeons of Northfleet & Gravesend 8
Doris & the Ducks 15
Kiki & Caesar and Captain Flint 23
A Parliament of Show-Off Rooks 30
One For Sorrow 40
Bird Whistles 46
Rhode Island Reds 51
Of Canaries & Coalmines 58
Fantails & Finches on Silk 66
Ultra-Short & Shaped 71
Weddings & Woodpigeons 79
Theft in Lord Darnley's Woods 87
The Fuse Box in the Coal Cupboard 95
Not a Patch on Going Hopping 104
Waiting for Womanhood 113
The Peep Toe Shoes 121
A Need For Plumed Horses 125
A Conspiracy of Ravens 135
The Truth Behind Plagues of Parakeets 142
Birds of Prey 148
The Very First Paddyfield Warbler 156
Miss Sands and the Swan 165
When Your Face Doesn't Fit 172
A Bird Called Kairo 179
Sid Strong & Ducks in Flight 188
Recalling Bluebirds 198
Never on the Never-Never 206
A Bird In The Hand 217
Appreciating the Cottage Homes 224

A Cage Fit for Eagles

Cage birds were once the pet of choice as far as the working classes of London and the South East were concerned. These days you might even call them Estuary Pets. Easy to keep, unlikely to offend the neighbours and certainly cost effective as far as food was concerned. There were even songs written about them such as the once celebrated Music Hall ditty about the couple doing a moonlight flit – *My old man said follow the van and don't dilly dally on the way.* The story-teller is the wife who walked behind the cart with the family pet and the popular melody itself would certainly be familiar with most who now qualify for a government pension.

A hundred years ago statistics estimate that every second household kept a cage bird of some kind and the craze began a long time before that if Pliny the Elder is to be believed. He laid the responsibility at the feet of Marcus Laenius Strabo of the Order of the Knighthood at Brindisi who, he wrote, began the practice of `imprisoning within bars wild creatures that Nature had assigned to the open sky'. He then went a step further and outlined the excesses some of his fellow Romans indulged in, citing an actor called Clodius Aesop who preferred his birds roasted, particularly favouring those that whilst alive had spoken in human voices. Pliny was scandalised, seeming to view this culinary treat as some kind of minor though hard to categorise form of cannibalism. Whether or not the vogue for pet birds started with the Romans is of course debatable but the craze was definitely trending in Europe in the early seventeen hundreds when French Huguenot weavers descended en masse upon London bringing their songbirds with them. And when I was a child the fashion was still alive and well in the streets of working class Gravesend and Northfleet and if my mother was to be believed the feathered friend of choice was then the Linnet. This relative of the Finch family was either routinely trapped in the wild or bred specially for sale in local pet shops and highly prized for its singing ability. It is likely that the male bird was especially sought after because of its colourful plumage although for some inexplicable reason the colours were slow to appear when caged. My mother decided that this peculiarity was almost certainly because they pined for their freedom, dreamed of soaring high into the Kentish sky – in other words it was a definite symptom of avian depression. Well she didn't quite put it like that but nevertheless she could have been right.

Although I know that we were a linnet owning family when my parents first married and moved into York Road it wouldn't be completely accurate to say that I actually remember Bobby, the bird itself. In fact by the time I was aware enough to take any interest in him he had already been given his freedom. This was in the hope that once restored to the wild he would grow a bright plumage and learn to sing rather than huddle on his perch in a woebegone and guilt-inspiring manner whilst conspicuously moulting. The only tangible evidence of Bobby himself was his empty cage, fashioned from slim lengths of bamboo and undeniably attractive. I wasn't allowed to play with it in case I did it some damage and it was stored in the cupboard under the stairs on a hook above the coal bunker awaiting his replacement.

Years were to pass before birds of any variety were to once more share the kitchen of number 28 with us. Although my brother was to become a firm ornithology enthusiast, birds either as pets or in the wild was not a subject I gave much thought to. However, I found it vaguely interesting when my favourite teacher Mr Will Clarke revealed that local author of some note, Charles Dickens, was said to have at one stage kept a pet Raven and Winston Churchill was a parrot fancier owning a Macaw called Charlie. My young brother, on the other hand was already wont to comment on the bamboo cage above the coal bunker from time to time, wistfully wondering if it would hold an eagle. Well he was only five years old at the time of that query and the only eagle he had actually seen was that which graced the front page of a recently launched boys' comic book. Still young enough to be easily confused and mostly bereft of reading skills he actually believed for a time that the popular periodical was some kind of Bird Fanciers' Weekly and even planned to name any future eagle he might own, Dan Dare in honour of the front page hero. Once he graduated from the first raft of Early Readers provided by St Joseph's Primary School it was with some embarrassment that he hastily tossed aside this particular notion though not the comic in its entirety. The first issue had been released in April 1950 following a huge publicity campaign and for a number of years it was enormously popular with boys between the ages of seven and sixteen providing a range of popular stories together with news and sports items.

Destined as he was to eventually emerge as a Bird of Prey fancier the green and grey budgerigar would not have been Bernard's first choice when it came to feathered companions and it is more than likely that a compromise was reached with my mother. She only capitulated regarding becoming a bird owner in the first place because the Bennetts of Buckingham Road had recently become the proud owners of Richie who, if their Joan was to be believed, had already learned to say his name. A week or two later our own bird, purchased from the pet shop in Queen Street, Gravesend, would have also been known as Richie if that popular budgie name had not already been bestowed upon the Bennett's bird. Instead, a further compromise was reached and ours was henceforth known as Ricky.

Without further ceremony the bamboo cage was retrieved from its place under the stairs, carefully wiped of coal dust and Ricky was installed. When Old Nan dropped in for tea and conversation a day or two later she said that we should have got him from the market because everybody knew that's where the best talkers were to be found and it was her belief that there was no real alternative. She would not be persuaded that Gravesend market did not go in for pet birds and said if that was the case it was a poxy excuse for a market if ever there was one. The fact that he had set us back the not inconsiderable sum of fifteen shillings and sixpence was further cause for derision because back in her day `them birds was ten-a-penny down Club Row' which was nice and handy to her East End childhood home. Well all that information was only if she was to be believed and often it turned out that she was not.

4

Ricky was not an immediate success at once displaying a hostile attitude towards his surroundings when he set about demolishing the bamboo cage that now hung in a corner of the kitchen above the shelf where the wireless lived. My mother was perplexed and said that Bobby the linnet had been a bird of a far less destructive nature and had always been as good as gold in the very cage that Ricky was fast destroying. Mrs Bennett advised that budgerigars had different beaks to those of linnets and should always be kept in wire cages and quite apart from that they liked toys. Our Ricky should be provided with a miniature mirror she advised because their Richie had one and these days you couldn't stop him talking. He said all manner of things and had them all in stitches.

A wire cage was investigated at Rayners in Northfleet High Street because at the pet shop in Gravesend they turned out to be Very Dear. But the Rayners variety were not exactly cheap either and so while the idea was given more consideration a mirror with a pink plastic trim was acquired and handed over to Ricky with a great deal of ceremony. But he was growing more recalcitrant by the day and showed not the slightest interest. Bernard and I took turns sitting beside him enunciating sound bites in the hope that he would emulate them but he seemed to be quite averse to `Ricky's a pretty boy' and `What a clever bird' no matter how often and how slowly these mini-bites were demonstrated to him. My grandmother said we'd definitely been sold a pup and that our bird was a pig in a poke and thus managed to completely confuse Bernard who was still at an age when he was inclined to take things adults said completely literally.

In a final act of desperation and having very recently added School Dinner Lady to her raft of part time jobs my mother announced that she was now feeling flush enough to lash out and treat Ricky to a brand new Rayners wire cage which came equipped with a bell for him to play with. It had not completely escaped her attention that the Bennett bird was a keen bell ringer though the noise at tea-time was enough to drive you to Colney Hatch. What with the new cage, the bell and the very latest in best bird seed with added oil to encourage the acquisition of speech she felt that our Ricky would very soon be making giant strides in every direction. But he continued to make very slow progress, showed no interest in being allowed out to occasionally fly around the room, refused to learn his name, found the new bird seed unpalatable and demonstrated complete indifference towards campanology. Overall he was not a total success and my mother was overheard to confide to her sister Mag that if there was one thing that gave her the pip, it was being forced to sit and listen to Grace Bennett listing all the new tricks that their Richie had learnt since she last drank tea with her. She just couldn't stop blowing his trumpet and when all was said and done he was only a bird.

So when poor Ricky was found deceased at the bottom of his cage one Sunday morning she clearly found it something of a relief and was not keen on replacing him. Once he had been buried with due ceremony beneath the only flowers in our garden, stolen from Lord Darnley's woods, the wire cage was cleaned and hung in the cupboard under the stairs without undue comment. After a while Bernard divulged that even though there was not to be an immediate successor to the wayward Ricky it was certainly a very good idea to keep the cage. When I asked him why he paused for a few seconds before adding that you never knew when it would come in useful and wanted to know if I thought it would be possible to keep an eagle in it – just a small eagle perhaps, one that was well behaved. I said I didn't know very much about eagles.

The Pigeons of Northfleet & Gravesend

Budgies and canaries, linnets and lovebirds were definitely not for all who lived in working class communities such as ours. In general they appealed to women rather than men and the male members of linnet owning households were definitely not as conspicuous in their enthusiasm for them as their wives. My grandmother thought that as far as birds were concerned you couldn't go past a parrot because they were a different matter, spending as much time out of their cages as within and definitely having the gift of speech. But you had to think carefully before becoming an owner because for one thing the cage itself would set you back a fair few bob and that was a fact and in any case you never knew with parrots with them prone to being delicate. You might spend a lot only to have the bugger drop dead on you. However, should you be lucky enough to be blessed with one of a sturdy constitution it might even see you out. Her Edgar's Uncle Snowball had inherited one before the turn of the century that had already seen its previous owner out and lived on for years after Snowball himself had succumbed to the perils of navigating that steep flight of stairs outside The Empire Tavern one Friday evening. A cheaper option when it came to men of course were pigeons and you generally found most men were partial to them.

Aunt Mag later told my mother that Snowball had been well and truly in his cups at the time of his demise.

My mother said anyhow bugger how long they lived because what was more concerning was the language they could come out with and it wasn't natural. Because I had yet to become well-acquainted with a parrot I thought she meant that they were multi-lingual which to my mind would be an asset in case you happened to come across someone needing help in the High Street who only spoke French or German. You could then take them home for a quick translation and become known locally as extremely helpful to foreigners. It might even be more convenient for all concerned to take your parrot with you when shopping. None of the adults in our community seemed all that kindly disposed towards foreigners of course, my mother and her sisters in particular.

It was to be some time before I would discover that the language of parrots had little to do with translation and anyway by then I had already turned my attention to pigeons, birds that every child in the area was familiar with because Old Nan was right and if there was a household pet that men were keen on it was definitely the pigeon, both homing and racing, not that I understood the difference. Mr Bassant next door had built what he said was a Pigeon Cree at the end of his allotment bordering The Old Rec, alongside Northfleet cemetery and he was always very keen to explain that his birds were Racing Homers and they could cover nearly a thousand miles in one sweep if necessary. The Cree looked very much like a garden shed to me and indeed he had reserved a space inside for his gardening tools and the wheelbarrow that he pushed laboriously up Springhead Hill twice a week full of vegetables. There was a big, open, window-like space along one side and above it was a special platform with little holes where the birds took off and landed again to enter their nesting places. All his birds had names and when he spoke to them he did so softly and lovingly, caressing them like babies. His favourites were Donald and Ridley because they could take off vertically, rising from the wooden platform with no hesitation and soaring up to meet the currents and eddies above before twirling atop of the whirlpools of air. Then they looked for all the world like miniature aerial fighters, the Spitfires we all recalled so vividly from a few years previously, tipping their wings and twisting triumphantly one to another. His girls, Betsy and Bella, Florence and Freda were more hesitant which he told us was female behaviour and sometimes they needed encouragement to follow their brothers and venture into the wide arc of sky above the marshland of the Estuary. Then he held them one after another close to his face and whispered to each and almost seemed to kiss each beak before the bird, though initially unwilling, suddenly fluffed up her breast feathers and decided to fly.

Sometimes after school Molly and I, at times accompanied by Pat Turner who lived in a cottage very close to the Old Rec Allotments, visited Old Mr Bassant, taking with us a replacement lemonade bottle of cold tea and instructions from his wife as to when she expected him home for his liver and bacon. He told us how clever his birds were and how when he sometimes took them all the way to Dover to visit another Pigeon Fancier, and released them there, by the time he got back to Northfleet in the evening all of them would have found their way home. We wanted to know how they knew their address and why they didn't get muddled up and perhaps end up in

Swanscombe or Greenhithe and Mr Bassant said they used the position of the sun to determine the proper direction for flight. But he didn't know how they fared if it was a rainy day not that it deterred them because they never once went to the wrong allotment and he knew for a fact there were allotments in Swanscombe. On the way home Molly said that to a bird Swanscombe must look much the same as Northfleet from the air and she for one was impressed. She was going to ask Mr Will Clarke about it the next day at school.

Mr Clarke said he was pleased we were taking an interest in pigeons because the Romans had used them to carry messages more than two thousand years before and in fact Julius Caesar had found them invaluable during his conquest of Gaul. Then Billy Elliott who always seemed to know more than anyone else in the class added that the Greeks sometimes used them to carry the names of victors of various Olympic events to other cities. Mr Clarke said that yes, indeed, that was absolutely true and well done Billy. We were all impressed then especially when he added that he might speak to Mr Cook the headmaster about considering the idea of us having some school pigeons. We might find them more interesting than the cage full of mice in the corner of the infants' room and we could have a roster for their care. In fact it never happened but it was a nice idea.

At the library in London Road the children's librarian revealed that it might sound unbelievable but these astonishing birds had always been much more reliable than the postal service and carrier pigeons could accomplish in a few hours what freight services took more than a day to do. Some of them flew at more than sixty miles an hour and never, ever lost their way. Having learned all of this for a time Molly and I were full of enthusiasm for joining a Pigeon Fancier's Club but it turned out that to become members you had to be sixteen years old and so then we began to lose interest especially since my mother said in her opinion they were Dirty Smelly Blighters and she wouldn't want them in the back bedroom like some she wouldn't name. She was referring to Aunt Elsie's George from the Tooley Street sweet shop who had several birds living in their tiny attic room that he called his pigeon loft alongside extra cartons of cigarettes and tall bottles of Sherbet Lemons bought whilst the price was low. He wasn't as friendly as Old Mr Bassant but he did tell us about a famous bird that saved the lives of dozens of French soldiers during The First World War. It was called Cher Ami which was French for Dear Friend and had carried a message across enemy lines during a battle. The bird was shot in the chest and lost most of the leg to which an important message was attached but it did not stop flying, continuing even through poison gas. Later Cher Ami was awarded a medal for heroism called The Croix de Guerre which was French for The Cross of War. I wondered if the injured leg ever healed but Aunt Elsie's George didn't know and in any case he was becoming tired of the conversation and I never found out and was never taken into the loft to view the birds. My grandmother said that was because he thought I might be light-fingered as far as the stored sherbet lemons were concerned.

Typically, once he became aware of my now waning interest in pigeons my father came up with a great deal of information and this was one of the reasons that prevented me from asking his opinion on some matters. His explanations were generally of the lengthy and elaborate variety. But on this particular Sunday lunchtime, after carving up a piece of rather fatty lamb which I was eyeing suspiciously, he started to tell me about the Dickin Medal which he said was the equivalent of the Victoria Cross but for animals. I was cautiously more interested and so I listened. Apparently the first such award was given to a carrier pigeon. In February 1942 an RAF bomber was forced to ditch into the North Sea following a mission over Norway. The plane had been hit by enemy fire and now the crew of four had to try to survive in freezing waters. Luckily they had a secret weapon, a hen bird called Winkie, and so they set her free hoping she could fly home to Dundee which was a place miles away in Scotland, and alert their colleagues at the base. Winkie flew a hundred and twenty miles and was found covered in oil and exhausted by her owner who informed the RAF in Fife which wasn't Dundee but must have been nearby. The position of the downed plane was then able to be calculated using the time difference between it going down and the arrival of the bird in the place called Fife. A rescue mission was then launched and the four men were found within half an hour. They would certainly have died without the help of the pigeon so she became the toast of the base and a dinner was held in her honour. A few months later she became the first animal to receive the Dickin Medal 'For valour under extreme circumstances'.

Not too long after this conversation I read of an American bird called GI Joe who saved more than a thousand lives in a village that was about to be bombed and another called Mary of Exeter who was used time and time again to send top secret messages. I learned that there is an inscription on the medals awarded that says 'We Also Serve' which seemed completely appropriate. And a few years ago whilst visiting Bletchley Park with my daughter I found myself paying particular attention to the displays, exhibits and information concerning the valiant feathered fighters of World War Two whose heroic deeds seem so sadly incongruous when placed alongside the myriad of communication choices we now have. As long as we now have the correct connection platform we can now make mobile phone calls, send and receive text messages, send emails and contact all and sundry via Whatsapp and Facebook at the touch of a button. None of these choice options have quite the romantic appeal of the trusty carrier pigeon, however, fifty thousand of which were drafted into service in the 1940s to carry messages, deliver medicines and bring hope to situations that otherwise might have been hopeless.

Doris & the Ducks

There was definitely TB in my mother's family. It was a fact that nobody was inclined to dispute. On the other hand neither was it admitted because it seemed to cause embarrassment. My grandmother herself was largely hale and hearty apart from an enduring addiction to alcohol which at times ruptured what might have otherwise been cordial relations with her extended family. As for my grandfather, he had wisely abandoned all alcoholic treats after Baby Arthur met an early demise when accidentally suffocated by his inebriated parents at the age of seven weeks. So it was a Bad Heart that eventually shortened Edgar Constant's life just before the outbreak of war when it was rumoured that the threat of his only live son's Call Up papers hadn't made life any easier for him, but his wife lived stubbornly on until Christmas Eve 1965. At the very moment she eventually succumbed following a late night walk down to The Jolly Farmers at Crayford to buy a half bottle of gin, my nephew Merlin was being born twenty miles up-river in St Bartholemew's Hospital, Smithfield to his excited teenage parents, my brother Bernard and his wife Janice. So her daughters often commented that there must be a bit of their mother in Little Merlin and Janice fervently hoped there was not!

When war finally broke out, in spite of all the worry and concern about Edgar Constant Junior being called up to serve his country, in the event no papers actually arrived because he numbered among the several Constant children whose birth had never been registered in the first place. Old Nan was apt to be forgetful concerning such formalities if seasonal field work was uppermost in her mind and in August 1912 it had been hop-picking which was of course more important than the registration of a child's birth. This lapse meant that young Edgar was in the fullness of time free to give his entire attention to the wartime Black Market, not to mention become of enormous comfort to several local women who missed the company of their serving husbands. Should his presence in the byways and bars of Crayford and Erith cause undue comment his mother and sisters stalwartly maintained that Poor Young Edgar had more than done his bit having been a hero of Dunkirk in 1940 which was of course quite untrue.

The scourge of TB that had plucked several Constant daughters from life in the 1930s continued to plague the family into the next decade taking two more aunts shortly after they gave birth leaving Poor Little Violet and Poor Little Doris motherless. Violet preceded her cousin by several months and being the first grandchild found in such a position was embraced into the maternal breast of my grandmother who said she would take on her upbringing as long as her father chipped in with some readies from time to time. He, only too delighted to rid himself of the burden of a small baby, agreed immediately. Later when fate saw Little Doris in the same position my grandmother was reluctant to enter into another such arrangement. She wasn't as young as she used to be and although Little Violet, bless her heart, never gave her a day's worry, taking on another baby was out of the question. There would have to be a roster. Well, she didn't quite put it like that but the rest of the family became quite aware of the expectations.

So in 1942 cousin Doris began what was to become a regular passage through the families of her various relatives, usually remaining for several weeks before being passed on. Fortunately she was of a calm and placid nature and endured being treated as an unwanted human parcel with fortitude, growing from a small baby who rarely cried to a resilient pre-schooler who seldom required any special attention with what seemed like grim determination just as long as she was occasionally taken to feed ducks. Over time it became clear that of all her cousins she got on with Aunt Mag's Margaret a great deal better than the rest of us. Margaret was several years older than me and the clutch of Crayford cousins and had been a schoolgirl for a number of years, what's more she also had the added advantage of childcare experience in the form of caring for her own baby sister Ann. She became especially good at amusing Doris, never tiring of ministering to her fondness for ducks by taking her down to the creek to feed them and watching carefully that she did not stumble into the brackish water in her excitement. Doris came to love her dearly and when she caught sight of her, her large blue eyes would light up which certainly did not happen when she came across me because as my mother was wont to point out, she and I simply did not get on.

My dead aunt had been what my mother called a Good Knitter and a Fair Hand at crochet and once she became sick during her pregnancy she took the opportunity of improving these skills. I came to realise that my dislike of Doris was partly because she came equipped with at least half a dozen silk dresses trimmed with angora of which I was very jealous. To add insult to injury she was a rather beautiful child and the aunts were fond of comparing her to Shirley Temple, even wondering if she might grow to develop similar performing skills as the famous child star. Her appearance was constantly commented upon, in particular her astonishingly extravagant and golden curls that framed her face and fell gently around her neck making her resemble a Botticelli angel. The sum total of the attention she generated did nothing to endear her to me and I certainly did not look forward to her visits when for what seemed like an interminable length of time she shared my bedroom and my mother's attention. Even worse, because she was younger than me she also shared my pushchair and I definitely felt that her turns when we walked to Gravesend and back were longer than mine.

Walking around the market on Saturdays with Doris being pushed and me having to hold on to the side of the handle and not get lost resulted in rapid affirmation of my antipathy towards my unfortunate cousin. We could scarcely go a few yards it seemed before women of all ages would comment on the blonde tresses, the sapphire blue eyes, the long lashes and the dimples and the object of all this attention would gaze into each approving face, pink lips slightly apart, dimples indented and a coy smile upon her face. Some of the admirers would also look me up and down and make comment that for sisters we were not in any way alike were we? One woman enthusing over Doris, briefly glanced at me before saying that I was quite plain wasn't I? My mother simply laughed and said that Poor Little Doris was her dead sister's girl and that as for Jean, well you could never get her hair to curl no matter how hard you tried. Later she said she'd been a rude cow. That day, while some shrimps were being bought for tea I took the opportunity of pinching my greatly admired cousin on her plump little left leg and then got annoyed when instead of volubly complaining she simply gazed at me forlornly whilst the doll-like eyes half filled with tears.

All things considered I had no affection whatsoever for this particular cousin and the Doris feature that I most abhorred was definitely the Shirley Temple hair and probably that was because during the time I discuss, small girls with the look of the American superstar were universally revered. As for Doris herself she seemed largely unaware of how she was regarded which my mother attributed to the fact that her mother, Poor Phyllis, had also been of unblemished character and never was one to blow her own trumpet. In fact Doris was so little trouble to care for that had I been better able to tolerate her presence I think she would have been considered for permanent residence at our place. Her Achilles' heel was definitely her fondness for ducks and the feeding of them with bits of stale bread and so because she was so good and undemanding, after shopping in the market we would invariably make our way along the riverside until we found a group of eager feeders. Although I was wary of getting too close to their beaks, Doris was never happier than when surrounded by a dozen Mallard or Muscovy distributing sustenance and never seemed to mind them encircling her in what I felt was an ominous fashion. Under normal circumstances all stale bread available at our place was earmarked for the making of bread pudding every second Saturday but when my cousin was with us that routine was cast asunder because Bless Her Little

Heart she enjoyed the duck feeding so much. Furthermore, when all was said and done, the Poor Little Mite didn't have much in life so who could begrudge her that pleasure? Well, I could for one.

I very much begrudged her that paltry pleasure along with her infant daring as she stood encircled by antagonistic, waddling Anseriformes battling for bread without at any stage losing her nerve. The shared life we had to intermittently endure, I felt, would be easier for everyone if Doris was not quite as brave or quite as curly. There was not a lot I could do about her exasperating daring so I gave a great deal of attention to the much admired hair and came to the conclusion that we would have to play a game of hairdressers the very next time she came to stay.

I didn't have long to wait once Aunt Martha's Pat came down with Mumps causing them to withdraw from their place on the care roster. Doris was shunted back to York Road, Northfleet much sooner than anticipated looking more dazzlingly beautiful than ever with pretty pink Bakelite clips, a third birthday gift from her father, pinning her hair back from her ears. Bakelite toys and trinkets had been all the rage prior to the outbreak of war and at some stage I had inherited an unattractive grey swan originally belonging to Margaret that I was allowed to float in the zinc bath with me on Saturday nights in front of the kitchen stove. Doris, not understanding much about swans, believed it to be a duck and we often had disputes over whose turn it was to do the floating. She coveted the swan so much that I had taken to hiding it under my bed just to punish her for her existence. However one Saturday in June 1944 I surprised her with my sudden altruism when I handed it to her to play with and even my mother noted approvingly that I was being very unselfish and she was proud of me. I went further and generously announced that Doris could take it to bed with her because I was a big girl now, having recently had my fourth birthday. Doris warmly thanked me managing to look only a little bit uneasy as she did so.

It was halfway through the following morning when my mother was preoccupied with making the Sunday dinner rice pudding that I suggested the new game which involved removing a pair of nail scissors from the manicure set my mother's long deceased fiancé Fred had given her then retiring to the end of the yard beside the entrance to the Anderson shelter. Doris followed just a little cautiously, the grey Bakelite swan beneath her right arm. Annoyingly she seemed determined to be more of a paragon of virtue than usual which was possibly because my mother had promised a walk to Springhead for duck feeding that afternoon just as long as both of us Behaved. I asked her if she would like to play hairdressers and she shook her head vigorously and held the swan just a little closer so I asked if she would like to keep the Bakelite swan when she left us. Doris nodded twice and turned anxiously towards the back door where she could hear my mother reassuringly banging saucepans and singing Molly Malone. Pulling her towards me I said she could keep the toy and it would be hers for ever just as long as we could now play hairdressers. I added that although we called the swan a swan it was in reality a duck, just a different kind of duck. She looked slightly more interested and as I moved above her with the nail scissors and sliced awkwardly through the uppermost golden ringlet she hugged the swan across her chest and whispered that she wanted very much to keep it because ducks were her favourite things and she loved them more than she loved God. Hissing at her to keep as still as she could I denuded her of what Old Mr Bassant next door had once referred to as her crowning glory as fast as possible. We then both stared at the triangular heap of coiled hair glistening between us in a kind of horrified hypnotised silence. Doris rocked slowly back and forth and although I had expected her to cry I noticed that her eyes were totally dry.

She only began to cry several minutes later when my mother came to investigate why we were being so quiet and good. And then so did I, heaving shuddering sobs as I explained that I had only done what Doris had asked me to do because she wanted to play hairdressers and she was no good with the scissors. Her hair had only suffered I explained because I was the one who was better with the scissors – simply because I was older. The game itself was definitely not my idea. I said nothing about the Bakelite swan and Doris did not argue when later I decided not to let her keep it after all. My mother was so angry that we were not taken to feed the ducks that afternoon after all which of course hurt Doris much more than it hurt me. She had never before known her Dear Little Niece to be so naughty and it was clear she was learning bad ways from somebody. I immediately agreed and suggested that maybe it was Margaret. Doris was still crying and said nothing at all and my mother simply gave me a very strange look.

Kiki & Caesar and Captain Flint

There has never been any doubt that parrots are exotic, having more than a hint of mystery and glamour about them without even having to try. Parrots carry the promise beneath their showy plumage of pirate ships and tattoo parlours, marine treasure and bottles of rum. To catch sight of one is to instantly perceive a flash of an alien land, a fast flourish of the ocean or even just a whiff of the murky estuary waters as they meet the Gravesend shoreline at the conclusion of a long journey. Parrots are pushy, more assertive than they need to be and invariably extravagantly gaudy. For those in the process of acquiring a bird companion they suggest bargain basement economy but will, as my grandmother warned, cost you an arm and a leg not to mention the fact that they could be fussy eaters and needed sturdy cages.

The only parrot I came across when growing up belonged to an elderly man who wore an ancient navy Guernsey and a cap and carried a khaki knapsack. I called him The Old Policeman and later learned that he had never been allied in any way to the Kent County Police Force but had spent most of his working life as a Thames Fisherman with a leaning towards eels and bass. It was rumoured to have been his brother who had left him the parrot when he died of the Pox and my mother hoped that the original owner had at least travelled further afield than the waters around Gravesend, perhaps even to China.

There was nothing exceptional apparently about eels and bass but plenty to get excited about when it came to China because the people living there were well and truly foreign and had funny habits. At the age of four I knew nothing about foreign places except that they were a very long way away which was fortunate because foreigners seemed more than anxious at the time to deluge the people of North Kent with bombs. Their latest nasty visitations were coming in the form of Doodlebugs that made even the grown-ups nervous. It was a long time before I met anyone from China and was in a position to judge the funny habits.

The parrot lived in a heavy-looking cage that swung gently in the window of a boarding house in West Street. The window was bigger than you might expect and hung with grimy grey net curtains. The unusual dimensions were because the house had been a shop and once upon a time had sold brown shrimps at threepence a pint, fresh from the Bawley boats. You could also at times get herring and haddock to take home for tea which they smoked in a yard out the back. There were still a few West Street shops left in those latter years of the war, one of them sold parts for bicycles and torch batteries and cans of oil and seemed to attract male customers only like my Uncle Harold. In fact it was he who told me that the bird in the window was a Macaw and so likely to live for a hundred years. He had just purchased what he said was an inner tube that he had been unable to come across in Crayford or Erith no matter how hard he'd looked and that was because of the war causing shortages. The bird came from South America he said which was most likely quite close to China I suggested and he agreed. His wife, Aunt

Mag looked proud of him and observed that Harold knew most things and if she ever wanted to find out something she always asked him first. Uncle Harold would smile at her then and squeeze her shoulders and instead of calling her Mag, which was her name when she wasn't being Margaret, he called her Croosh because she was crucial to him. My mother always said later that Harold was a Dopey Sod if ever she knew one and didn't know his arse from his elbow and as for his Mag being crucial to anyone well that was laughable that was. In this case, however, I thought he was probably quite correct about the parrot. It was an astonishingly and intensely blue and gold bird and looked for all the world as if it had been exposed to bright dyes such as the ones Aunt Maud got from Woolworths and used when she did a makeover of her shoes. In fact it was so colourful it was hard to take your eyes off it, and the harder you looked at it, the more it seemed to preen and straighten itself and look as important as it could possibly manage within the confines of the cage that had more than likely cost so much, even though it looked a bit on the small side.

West Street in those days differed substantially from later when the demolitions that took place to widen it so as to accommodate the one way system had taken place. In the 1940s it was still narrow and infused with an air of architectural antiquity though most of the old shops had already turned themselves into what my mother said was slum housing where a number of families had to share a the lavatory in the yard which just wasn't right. Old Nan thought she'd not say that if she'd seen the state of the area when Suttis Alley and Mermaid Court were still standing quite close to the baker where we now bought our custard tarts. In her opinion to call the West Street houses slums meant she didn't know what a slum was. After this kind of exchange there would follow a few minutes of hostile muttering between them about who was correct.

On the north side of the street where the parrot lived there were, unlike later, still plenty of pubs, a number of which advertised Whitebait Suppers and sometimes if several of my aunts had come to town together for a Saturday afternoon shopping expedition they would go inside for a quick one, leaving me and my cousins in the charge of Margaret who as I have said before, had a responsible nature. If one of the uncles was with them he might stay behind for a second quick one when they proceeded to the market. Either way once we children had demolished the packets of crisps we were given to share we progressed further along the street towards what I now inside my head called The Chinese Parrot House and stared at the bird who stared back curiously, doing nothing very much even when Pat banged on the window to try to startle it into some kind of action. Margaret said that well trained parrots went out with you and sat obediently on your shoulder. You could even take them on the 480 bus she said and she had seen people getting off with them at the stop outside Dartford market. I somewhat doubted that because although I had often seen dogs on buses I had never at any stage seen a parrot nor indeed any other kind of bird. Despite Margaret's insistence that seemed to imply that parrots were happiest when sitting on the shoulders of their owners the elderly man I called The Old Policeman was never to be witnessed with the Macaw in that position which was disappointing.

One exciting day when my mother and I were on our way back from the West Street baker with freshly baked huffkins in the shopping basket, we happened upon the next door Bassants' adopted daughter Ena who was emerging from The Chinese Parrot House with a key in her hand and a determined-to-ignore-us look on her face. But my mother wasn't to be ignored that day. After some discussion it turned out that Ena was currently employed on a part-time basis by the elderly landlady who was in need of help to clean the rooms and brush down the stairs every second week because of her rheumatism. There were five lodgers in the house, all of them men so the lavatory arrangement, which of course my mother brought up immediately as a topic for discussion, did not pose a lot of problems. There was no food provided so no meals to cook and clean up after and the sheets on the beds were only changed every third week because when all was said and done men generally were not fussy and didn't notice things like grimy sheets nor clean ones for that matter. All things considered Ena felt it wasn't too bad a little wartime job and a lot better than the factories where you had to clock in and out. There my mother agreed and told the story of her own sister who had nearly had the nasty accident at Vickers and was lucky she wasn't killed. Within reason Ena could choose her own hours and there was a lot to be said for that and not a chance of nearly having a finger blown off or your hair caught in machinery or worse.

 Their conversation became more and more tedious so I started hopping on one leg and saying how much I liked the parrot in the window. With some encouragement the Bassants' Ena then agreed to take me into Old Reg

Cogger's room for a closer look at it because her Evelyn had loved it too when she went to work with her one day last week. My mother was doubtful and wondered if he would mind but Ena said with any luck he would be in The Shades until dinner time anyway and would never know. In actual fact he returned before expected with several bottles of beer in his khaki knapsack which seemed to confuse Ena who hastily explained that she had just brought the kiddy in for a few minutes to have a look at the bird. My mother added that in any case I was always as Good as Gold.

And that's how I came to learn that the bird's name was Caesar and he was only rarely let out of his cage on account of him having a Bugger of a beak on him and a temper to go with it. Rolling up the sleeve of his navy Guernsey Reg Cogger invited me to look at some of the damage Caesar had done when using the rogue beak to steady himself as he got around. Sometimes, he said, with the best will in the world Caesar would accidentally slip and be forced to use his beak to hold on which always resulted in something that looked very much like an intentional attack. I stood several respectful feet away from the cage and listened and tried as hard as I could to look as Good as Gold.

Ena and my mother melted back into the narrow entrance passage of the West Street house and Old Reg sat down in a wicker armchair and prepared himself a roll-up. When I asked if Caesar could speak he told me he could not only speak but swear like a trooper in four languages and sing God Save the King. So I took a small and cautious step or two back towards the cage again through the crowded little room waiting for the bird to do so but disappointingly he said nothing at all and neither did he sing. So I asked Old Reg if he ever took him on his shoulder onto the 480 bus and he said he didn't because of fear he might fly away and then he might never get him back though he wouldn't entirely discount the idea because you could in fact buy a special harness for taking birds out and about. Parrots like Caesar were worth a bob or two he told me and were splendid pets, in fact much better than dogs because they didn't need the walking. After the war, once goods were in the shops again he might get one of them there harnesses. That sounded like an excellent idea to me and I instantly decided that in the future, when I had a parrot of my own which I was definitely going to call Caesar, I would make sure that it never flew away on the 480 bus by buying it a harness.

In the years that would intervene before I ever became in a position to fulfil that promise to myself of acquiring a parrot, I made it a priority to give attention to these birds both factual and fictional. Not that many were to be found in the pet shops of Gravesend and Northfleet. When I was nine I only struggled through Treasure Island because of Long John Silver being a fellow fancier. Information was thin on the ground but my childhood world became suffused with justice when I stumbled upon Enid Blyton's Adventure series of improbable novels featuring Jack, Philip, Dinah, Lucy-Anne and... yes, Kiki the parrot! My future avian companion's name was rapidly changed from Caesar to – yes, of course – Kiki!

A Parliament of Show-Off Rooks

Bernard first spoke to me of the spectacle of roosting birds when he was still quite a small boy, perhaps five or six years old. He had been observed by an elderly neighbour sitting on the front doorstep as quiet and still as was possible in order to best monitor the comings and goings of sparrows and starlings and pigeons. He liked the starlings best of all with their brash certainty and their glossy and sometimes iridescent plumage, each struggling to be noticed as perhaps he longed to be himself. He wondered why they sometimes developed speckles of white about their feathers and why their bills were black in winter and yellow in summer but of course I couldn't tell him and neither could the neighbour. He enjoyed their noisy squabbling and told me that somewhere he had heard that they could learn to speak which was something I had never heard myself so I told him that was unlikely. What he liked most about them was their determination to be gregarious and their habit of flocking together as they headed for their communal roost. Before he totally changed his mind about egg collecting, one of their pale blue eggs was his first ornithological acquisition. He placed it gently into a fake nest he had made on the table beside his bed.

He learned from a library book called *Our Feathered Friends for Young Folk* that mid-winter was probably the best time for spotting an undulating flock just before the sun went down. He told me that this was known as a Murmuration and our closest one was probably along the line of poplars down by Gemmel's Farm adjacent to Springhead. If we were lucky, he said, we might see ten thousand or more at any one time.

My mother had long since decided that he was far too young to what she called Traipse around the countryside after bloody birds by himself and so she detailed me to go with him if he was to go at all. So that is how we came to be sitting on the side of a frozen ditch one early December evening on the edge of one of Mr Gemmel's ploughed fields. It was what my grandmother would have termed as cold as charity and although I was aware of every last degree of it, my brother was totally oblivious, hugging his pink knees and whispering that the concentration of birds we were about to see was because that habit served as a defence against falcons and hawks that would slaughter them in a blink of an eye. After a long silence within which I wondered how soon I would be able to persuade him that we needed to go home, he looked at me and asked if I thought it was exciting. I said Yes, I did because to say anything else would have seemed unnecessarily unkind.

And then it began. Slowly at first a tight sphere-like formation in the sky above us, expanding and contracting like an amorphous troupe of dancers then changing shape as if choreographed, each bird following the movement of its closest neighbours. The swarm was creating one complex shape after another, every one silhouetted against the rapidly darkening sky and each process of change astonishingly elegant.

Next day Mr Hammond, the shoe-mender of Shepherd Street, said when he was a boy some people kept starlings and they could be trained if you caught them young enough not only to do tricks but to talk. One he came across could mimic the human voice so well that folk turned around to see who was speaking. When Bernard went home to acquaint my mother with this piece of information, Old Nan who was on her third cup of Wednesday afternoon tea said she wouldn't give them house room because they were dirty buggers and inclined to shit all over the place. That seemed a bit odd to Bernard because if they were being kept in cages there would be a natural limit to the extent of this annoying habit. But in any case he didn't want to keep one at all so he did not think it worthwhile arguing about it.

I felt obliged to discuss with him a few days later that the Roost of starlings had been more interesting than I would have thought possible and following this admission over the next several months we wandered far and wide to witness similar winter evening exhibitions. Bernard even talked about the phenomena at school one morning at one of the inaugural Show & Tell demonstrations that were seeing their introduction into English primary schools in the 1950s. St Joseph's prided itself on being much more progressive than other local schools, particularly those with no religious affinity and therefore considered next to heathen. He was so enthusiastic that it was difficult for Sister Camilla to actually stop him talking which infuriated Anne Murphy who was detailed to follow him and was to talk about her pet rabbit which she had brought with her in a very smart pen bought from Rayners.

The following autumn Bernard stopped talking about Murmurations of starlings and began instead to discuss Rooks. He very much wanted to go to Cooling to witness a Roost. He told me that the flock would not be called a Murmuration and would be called a Parliament instead and furthermore although it was easy to confuse the Rook with the Crow the former was distinguished by greyish skin around the base of the bill in front of the eyes and that in any case their feathered legs looked shaggier than those of the Crow. I bore all this in mind and promised never to confuse them.

Rashly I undertook to take him to the Rook Roost at Cooling at the first opportunity and did so only because I recalled the walks I had done with my father whilst he was still alive, walks that seemed interminably long at the time, along the Thames and Medway Canal to the marshes at Cliffe where I was told we trod in the very footsteps of Charles Dickens when he was a boy. When Bernard next went to the library the children's librarian gave him permission to borrow from the Ornithology section in the adult library where they had seven or eight volumes by various authors that told you all you could possibly want to know about birds, including Rooks. He learned that they were highly gregarious and that males and females bond for life, that to farmers they were a nuisance because of their habit of decimating crops and most exciting of all, their spectacular aerial displays in autumn had to be seen to be believed. So he became intent upon observing this for himself and spoke non- stop about how exciting it was going to be when we finally found ourselves in the village of Cooling with the Roost itself, as our grandmother would say, within spitting distance! In the meantime he offered several times to share his newest information at Show & Tell time at school but was told that the subject matter he suggested wasn't appropriate. He was only seven years old at the time and therefore extremely hurt.

The journey plan was finally made in the first term of the school year in September when an outbreak of Measles locally ensured that being absent would mean he wasn't noticed. I was recovering from a rather nasty attack of Chicken Pox and had not been at school for three weeks and our mother was conveniently detailed to be at Old Nan's place in Crayford by eight am to look after Little Violet while Nan's feet were attended to at the local hospital. She might be late back and we were therefore to get our own tea of fish and chips with the shiny half-crown left on the kitchen table. She was temporarily feeling flush because of an extra day or two worked the previous week for Mrs Lovell of Darnley Road. In addition she undoubtedly felt a certain amount of working class guilt at not being home to make sure we ate two slices of bread and what was always called Butter followed by a home-made rock cake or two. We took the rock cakes with us, wrapped in newspaper.

Purloining odd coins from the Toby jug above the kitchen stove provided a further cash injection for the bus fare into Gravesend but after that we would have to walk if we wanted to be sure of fish and chips later. In any case it was generally unwise to ask clippies to give change for half-crown pieces because they were almost honour bound to be rude simply because we were children which would only draw the attention of other passengers towards us. I felt a slight unease in any case about being a child because in those days as far as bus fares were concerned you stopped being one at the age of fourteen unless you were on your way to school preferably in school uniform. I had recently celebrated my fourteenth birthday.

As fate would have it, when we got to the bus stop opposite the Catholic church nosy Mrs Newberry was already in the queue poised ready to cross examine us with what passed as a look of polite interest on her face. Mrs Newberry had replaced The Bassants Next Door when they went to live in Burch Road Rosherville with their adopted daughter Ena. She was very keen on hand washing and stayed up late at night making sure that her family had the cleanest shirts, frocks and socks in the neighbourhood. My mother said that it wasn't natural and to mark her words because her hands would suffer something terrible in the long run. I found myself staring at her hands as she predictably wanted to know where we were off to so early on a Wednesday morning. I said I was taking my brother to the new Ear Clinic at the hospital and wanted to get there before the rush. My mother had discussed over the fence with her as she pegged out endless lines of newly washed garments that my brother suffered dreadfully with his ears which was true because he did. So Nosy Mrs Newberry made sympathetic noises and said she understood bad ears only too well as her hubby, Charlie had been a sufferer in his childhood and had ended up deaf on one side because back in those days there was no new Ear Clinic to attend, no matter how early you got up to go there.

Then, as we boarded the bus and seated ourselves, Bernard couldn't help himself and announced that we were also going to Cooling for the Rook Roost. I added that we might do but only if time permitted and his ears were not too bad and I kicked his shin violently. In a smaller voice he began to explain to her that rooks were very interesting and had surprisingly powerful beaks and that sometimes they walked around the fields in huge steps and sometimes they hopped just like sparrows but of course she wasn't listening. When we arrived in the town, however, she was still aware of us enough to prompt us to get off the bus at the stop closest to the hospital which we didn't really want to do but did anyway and thanked her for the reminder. As we headed south towards the canal, past the shops on the main road, still not open, my brother observed that possibly pretending to be on a hospital visit had not been very good idea. It quite quickly began to seem like a very long walk and we had to ask directions on a number of occasions from people out with their dogs. The men were generally taciturn but when we approached the occasional woman she was invariably helpful though curious and wanted to know where we were heading and why.

The winter sun grew higher in the sky and once we managed, after what seemed a very long time, to get into the marshland environs of Cliffe and Cooling I began to feel more positive. I was again remembering the many walks I had done with my father in previous years before he was so suddenly snatched from life when Bernard was still a pre-schooler. Importantly I said I was completely familiar with the marshland route and why, and Bernard was impressed and even said he wished he'd been old enough to come with us back then. Further enthused I began to recite the history lesson I had been subjected to on one such perambulation and told him that Cooling, where we were now heading, got its name from a Saxon word which meant Cow and that the Romans had once occupied the area which was a fact because in 1922 on a nearby farm a Roman kiln had been found and it contained a great deal of Roman pottery.

We sat by the roadside to eat the rock cakes which were not the best that my mother, who was by no means much of a baker, had ever produced. Bernard did not seem to mind and neither did he object when I pointed out that the construction of Cooling Castle was started in the thirteen hundreds and that the church featured in *Great Expectations* by Charles Dickens. He did ask who Charles Dickens was though but I decided not to subject him to a trip to the churchyard to see the little tombstones that were supposed to be Pip's brothers and sisters as it was rather depressing.

The walk became interminable and when we came across a shop beside some newly built houses we decided to buy lemonade and Smith's Crisps to sustain us with some of the money that had been reserved for fish and chips. After all, Bernard said, we could always simply buy chips when we got back to Gravesend because as far as he was concerned, chips were the best part of fish and chips. I agreed because there seemed to be no earthly reason why we needed fish. The woman behind the counter said she thought we looked Done In and Bernard said we were going to the Rook Roost and had walked all the way from Gravesend. She said we should have taken the bus to High Halstow and we should be sure to catch the bus on the way back.

It was becoming late in the afternoon by the time we reached Northward Hill and found the Saxon Shore Way where my brother insisted we needed to be to get the best view. A dog walker told us we were now in a good place to observe the Roost and so we sat exhausted on the edge of a coppice, Bernard complaining that his legs were hurting quite badly. I nodded, wondering where the bus stop was and how I might recognise which was the best bus to catch back to Gravesend. It would not be a very satisfactory end to the day to find ourselves in Rochester or Chatham for instance. And while I was contemplating the possible minor calamities that might yet be in store for us Bernard clutched my arm and whispered that it was about to begin. So in the early winter dusk all thought of bus timetables and routes were forgotten and we sat mesmerised as the red and grey sky that stretched endlessly over the marshland became inky with a myriad of birds wheeling and gliding in groups. As one but in their thousands they played to the gallery, distracting us, demanding our attention and performing a series of spectacular synchronised movements, diving, rolling and tumbling unrestrained against the clouds just as the Springhead Starlings had done only with more abandon, as if taking part in some strange and dazzlingly accomplished avian ballet.

On the way back towards the road through the rapidly descending darkness Bernard said that the Rooks were much better than the Starlings and I asked him why. He thought it was because they were better at letting us see what they could do. Doing what Sister Camilla at school had warned his class against – showing off, because it was her firm opinion that nobody admires a show off. Nonetheless it was all but impossible not to admire the rooks.

Somehow or other we found the bus that went to Gravesend and then we only had to walk to Northfleet. We bought chips and doused them liberally with salt and vinegar and Bernard told me that he greatly admired the Show-Off Rooks and that the day had been the very best day of his life.

One For Sorrow

We suffered a plague of hostile Magpies for two or three years in Kohimarama when my children were growing up and at one stage my young daughter became distinctly uneasy at the thought of going outside. Sinead was not generally of a nervous disposition but at six and seven years old she was on the small side and the Magpies, as with everything else introduced to New Zealand by enthusiastic early settlers, had taken full advantage of an environment that was at odds with itself being both quasi-tropical and temperate. It was those self-same Pacific conditions that had allowed English Gorse to achieve the gigantic proportions that rendered it unrecognizable to the average Englishman and meant that the standard house rat had to be seen to be believed. The positive aspect of the massive Magpies at least ensured that Sinead's previous dislike of irritating Mynah birds was put into perspective. The latter were certainly aggressive at times but a dive-bombing Mynah was simply not in the same ballpark as a dive-bombing Magpie. Her older brother also wisely kept his distance from them but was not as voluble as to why.

Because we were actively engaged in home schooling at the time of this scourge, like my father before me who did not have a similarly valid excuse, I used the situation as a tool for education. With what can only be described as missionary zeal and modelling myself on the La Leche

League who were at the time preaching breast feeding with the same kind of fervour, I threw myself into the business of making sure that all available information about the feathered delinquents that stalked the flat roof of the house planning assaults should be made available to my two increasingly alarmed students.

They were encouraged to learn the verse that all English children were undoubtedly still aware of... *One for sorrow, two for joy, three for a girl and four for a boy. Five for silver, six for gold and seven for a secret never to be told...* which only mildly amused them. And we listened to Rossini's overture La Gazza Ladra endlessly over a week or more which they didn't seem to mind too much. This was years before the advent of the internet but it did not take them too long to discover that Thieving Magpies probably number among the most detested birds in the avian world and have consequently become attached to a raft of extraordinary superstitions. I was solemnly informed that the bird was the only one not to sing as Jesus died on the cross and was therefore immediately seen as evil. At a more practical level their habit of stealing and eating the eggs and young of other birds to supplement their diet did not win much support either.

Discovering that they have a natural attraction to shiny objects, a wide range of items was placed outside for them to choose from – pieces of kitchen foil, metal screws, glass beads and a silver ring bought years before in Portobello Road market. Predictably perhaps the only piece they selected was the ring, cherry picked and seeming to decide upon after circling it for several minutes, flying away then one of them returning to suddenly claim it. Sinead promised she would retrieve it just as soon as she discovered where our thieving trio secreted their horde but of course she was never able to do so. Seamus, predictably perhaps by then decided that what he wanted more than anything else was a pet Magpie and we determined that should he be able to somehow trap a chick he might well be allowed to keep it. There was not of course much chance of this but even so the promise was made, much to his father's horror. This opposition went back to when he was a child in Oamaru in the South Island and a neighbour had somehow or other come by a pet bird that he was now sure had been a Magpie but possibly might have been a Jackdaw. Either way he was terrified of it because it had a habit of pecking his ankles. The children assured him that their bird, should it ever eventuate, would be trained not to peck. Their father, still recovering from a range of animals he thought he had forbidden including a lizard called Eliza, a rat called Grendel, two rabbits called Enid Blyton and Beatrix Potter, and an angora goat called Cindy, looked doubtful. He seemed to have an aversion to anything with feathers and sadly, most things with fur unless they were cats – of which we at that time had three. He had not been a typical New Zealand child, always refusing to go to the circus because he decided it was dirty, even unhealthy. There seemed little likelihood under the circumstances that a Magpie might be slipped past him but Sinead told her brother not to give up hope because he worked long hours and it might be several weeks before he even noticed.

Meanwhile I was recalling the antics of the belligerent bird kept by Old Mrs Yates who at one time lived next door to one of my Crayford aunts. It was said to have arrived on the scene when Cyril her husband died and to make ends meet she had taken in a lodger called Dan who worked at Vickers and was said to be a sober, church-going bachelor. There was the standard confusion as to whether his feathered companion was a Magpie or a Jackdaw but what nobody argued about was that it was a Spiteful Blighter and somebody should wring its neck. It spent most of its time tethered by one scrawny leg to the chair Dan sat on at dinner time, poised to peck each passer-by. In the summer time Dan moved his chair outside onto the street so that the bird could exhaustively amuse itself with attacks on passing children heading for the shop that sold raspberry and lime Ice Suckers. He said its name was Mary and it meant no harm because it was merely playing a game.

 Within a short space of time Old Mrs Yates together with Dan and Mary became even more unpopular than Flash the Alsatian who lived opposite my aunt and had an equally alarming habit of hurling himself at the gate each time someone dared to pass. His owner said it was because he was named after Flash Gordon and just couldn't help himself and if you stood your ground he would do you no harm. Of the two aggressors I was possibly more intimidated by Mary. My aunt told my mother that there was more to the house next door than met the eye and she was convinced there was Hanky Panky going on because apart from anything else you could hear it through the bedroom wall on Sunday afternoons and she thought it ought to be reported to the Council. My mother said that at her age, and she must be sixty if she was a day, Mrs Yates should be past all that but my aunt said No, she wasn't and they were at it like rabbits. The reference to rabbits was perplexing to a seven-year-old so I mentioned it to my cousin Margaret who was fourteen – were Mrs Yates and Dan at it like rabbits? She looked horrified and said I shouldn't say such things so I didn't say it again but I still would have liked an answer.

Not very long after this exchange Mary the Magpie pecked my cousin Violet's leg one Sunday morning as she passed on her way to the shop for two ounces of loose tea. Violet didn't take kindly to the attack and rushed back to report the incident knowing very well that Old Nan wouldn't take kindly to it either. This resulted in a great deal of what was generally termed Argy Bargy with threats and raised voices and Dan the lodger being told that he'd feel the back of Nan's hand if her Violet, Poor Motherless Little Mite, ever had cause to complain again. Later it became common knowledge among first my aunts and then the rest of the street that although Dan was generally sober and sometimes went to church, a bachelor he was not because he had two wives, one in Wolverhampton and one in Norwich, both of whom had thrown him out because they couldn't abide Mary the Magpie.

Not long after that there must have been a complaint to the Council because Mrs Yates suffered the ignominy of an eviction notice which normally you only got if you didn't pay your rent or if you punched holes in the wall when you were drunk and were unlucky enough to be found out. My mother said it was on account of the bird but that couldn't have been correct because there was no regulation stipulating that you couldn't keep pets and even antagonistic ones like Flash were tolerated. Either way Aunt Mag maintained that although she was glad to see the back of them, the eviction was nothing to do with her and she had better things to do with her time than report people to the Council.

Once they moved on and were replaced by a family with four girls and two canaries, my Grandmother found herself in a better frame of mind about neighbours who kept birds though she said that Magpies were said to have drunk the blood of Satan and were therefore best avoided. It was terrible bad luck, she said, to have one hover above your house because it meant a death was about to happen but on the other hand if you should be on your way to a wedding and happen to see three of them that meant the couple about to be wed would have a happy future. And if you suffered from fits and could bear to catch one and eat it, you would be cured of that affliction at once, nothing was surer. This is something I might have paid heed to myself when later in life I developed Epilepsy but by then it had slipped my mind.

Bird Whistles

Young Harold was my oldest cousin and he and Young Leslie had often been mistaken for twins when they were small according to my mother. Well she should know because according to her she had all but brought them up when she went to live with her sister Mag after being thrown out of home for fighting with her sister, Maud. She always believed that it was Maud who should by rights have been thrown out because when all was said and done, it had been Maud who started the argument about who had used the last of the Amami Shampoo. But on that particular Saturday evening Old Nan had ordered her Edgar to throw Nellie out of the house without even a coat over her shoulders because she'd had a gutsful well and truly with the neighbours complaining that those Constant girls were always fighting. She had to walk every step of the way to Iron Mill Lane, because she didn't have a penny to her name. But far be it from her to complain and in the end the new living arrangements, because that's what they turned out to be, benefitted everyone. Mag was now free to take a job at Vickers which she had been champing at the bit to do because Nellie was only too happy to stay home and look after those dear little boys. Returning to the family home to resume working for their father delivering meat and fish was out of the question in any case. To be honest she was only too glad not to because she'd never really got on with

Toby the pony. Mag was going to give her a pound a week and that was good enough for her. There was good money to be made down at Vickers and no mistake.

This new arrangement was going to give her more time to give attention to Poor Fred and nobody could say he didn't deserve attention. She would now be able to visit twice a week if she so desired even if it did mean an inconvenient change of trains. Crayford to Waterloo then a half hour wait for the fast train to Godalming. Just a brisk walk then to the Sanitorium where Fred enjoyed the best rest and fresh air that Surrey could provide. Once he was well again they would re-schedule their wedding date. She would wear Mag's wedding dress and real orange blossom in her hair and the two of them would get as far away from Crayford and all the fighting and argy-bargy as was possible – perhaps even to Gravesend. 1930 was going to be the best year of her life.

So that's how my mother came to be what would now be termed the Prime Carer to Harold and Leslie Linyard, both still under two years old and often dressed alike and as people said, mistaken for twins, although of course in reality there was just over a year between them. In time the rift created by being thrown out of home was healed enough for conversation to take place between the main players which was a good thing. After a shaky start when Young Harold screamed persistently for his mother when she left the house with her hair tied up in a smart red turban telling him she would be back in the shake of a gnat's whisker, he settled down and accepted Aunt Nell as a substitute.

So it was my mother who pushed the boys all the way up Iron Mill Lane to the High Street shops and bought

Harold a magic bird whistle that had to be filled with water. The young assistant was very obliging and went out to the back of the shop and came back with it filled and in working order for him. It was yellow and she told him it was a Canary and showed him how to blow it hard to make it work. Once he worked it out he was delighted and made full use of it although his mother said that the noise drove her barmy. When Leslie got a little older my mother bought him one as well, a red one and said it was a Robin Redbreast. This did not please their mother either. It pleased their Aunt though and when the children began to appeal directly to her to mend their bumps and scrapes rather than Mag, it pleased her even more. And so Aunt Nell became much loved and remained at the house in Iron Mill Lane over a number of years and was still there when baby Margaret was born in 1933. Within a short space of time when Mag decided it was time she returned to Vickers, she duly took over the care of the new baby. She was there when Poor Fred died instead of getting better despite all the rest and fresh air and it was Mag who sat up at night with her when the sleeping pills gave her nightmares, and it was the children who made life bearable during daylight hours.

    Mag and Big Harold did the best they could for her state of mind and introduced her to Big Harold's brother from Wolverhampton, Big Leslie who rode a motor bike and was in the market for a wife. She found his habit of surreptitiously wiping his nose on his shirt sleeve offensive even though he only did it at the end of the working week when the shirt was imminently due to be washed. It would be true to say that there was not much love lost between her and Big Harold who she thought was for a number of reasons, a silly bugger. She disliked him for having a distasteful brother, for insisting on calling her sister Croosh rather than Mag or Maggie, for disciplining poor Young Leslie, a sensitive child, too harshly and for calling him John rather than Leslie. Maud, who had by that time married her George, moved to a house in Mayplace Avenue and given birth to Young Desmond, was wont to point out that my mother could be a mischief maker when she wanted to be. However, it was more important to Mag to have an on the spot carer for her three children than to spend too much time worrying about those who might make mischief, and so my mother remained in the small bedroom.

The children were more than happy with the arrangement although try as she might, my mother was unable to find a bird whistle for Margaret when she grew old enough to want one. Instead she knitted a full set of clothes for the doll called Pola that Margaret had been given for her third birthday. She was rather beginning to feel, however, that she should move away and would have done so already had it not been for Poor Fred's death because that had really knocked her for six. With these thoughts in mind perhaps she gave more of an appraisal than she would have ordinarily have done to the fellow motor cyclist, a friend of Big Leslie's introduced in The Jolly Farmers one Sunday afternoon – Bern, brought up in a Chatham orphanage, coming up to thirty years old and also on the lookout for a wife.

He wasn't a patch on her Fred of course but then she couldn't expect that could she? Not a man she was likely to grow to love with all her heart but then where had that got her in the past? Devotion and hope for the future had only tied her to grief and sorrow. He seemed a sober man, a man who did not use bad language, a man who had a library ticket and regularly went to Mass. She could do worse and it would do her no harm at all to go to Mass from time to time and there was nothing wrong with joining a library. She'd always enjoyed reading.

It was Young Harold who missed her most when she left and he kept the bird whistle for years. She in her turn always had a soft spot for him even when he grew up and worried about doing his National Service because Malaya seemed too foreign and too far away. He promised to bring her back a Love Bird, perhaps even a pair but somehow or other he wasn't able to. She was always suspicious of that Joan he got engaged to who was a Silly Cow and later threw him over for some reason. More fool her! She was happy when he met Sylvie from Hemel Hempstead and swiftly married her. You had to hand it to Sylvie because she was a very good cook and that suited Harold and she spent ten pounds a week on food. Ten pounds – no exaggeration! The first of their kiddies was little Wayne who looked so much like his Daddy. They had five in the end and went to live over Slade Green way so she didn't see much of them.

They did come down to Gravesend Market one Saturday afternoon though and it was Young Harold who spotted the bird whistles, made of yellow plastic. My mother bought one for little Wayne and was inordinately pleased when Young Harold told him Aunt Nell had given him one just the same when he was a little lad, and showed him how it worked.

Rhode Island Reds

It was my father who initiated the keeping of six hens and a rooster because just imagine having a plentiful supply of new-laid eggs not to mention the occasional home raised Chicken Roast? The manner in which he enthused had me hooked very quickly even though I had some doubts with regard to the Roast, infrequent though it was going to be and this was because when questioned he failed to explain that part of ownership even though I posed a fair few questions. In the end I decided that he could not really mean that we were eventually going to eat the birds because that was an easy enough question to answer and in any case we usually bought our Chicken Roasts already quite deceased and sometimes these days even oven prepared from the butcher at Christmas time. It saved a lot of trouble as far as I could see.

My mother was much slower to reach any agreement about the idea because she really did not like roosters and said they could be vicious. The rooster we eventually got was only four weeks old at the time we first owned him and was not vicious at all and she suggested that maybe he wasn't a rooster in the first place because he was nothing like Spiteful Stanley, the bird who had reigned supreme in the house in Maiden Lane, Crayford when she was a girl. My father told her he was most definitely a rooster and pointed out that his comb was already developing and was a healthy pink colour. We called him Cecil because of

Cecil Rhodes at least that's what I called him and that was because of Miss Biggs at school pointing to a pink bit on the globe and talking about Mr Rhodes very enthusiastically. I was told that our batch of fowl were Rhode Island Reds and American in origin, all supposedly Reliable Layers. I did not know if there was any real connection between Rhode Island and Cecil Rhodes but fancied that he may at one stage have owned the island. Cecil's six wives, and I mean our Cecil of course, were not supposed to have names because it was very difficult to tell one from another although I claimed ownership over the smallest one and named her, unimaginatively, Clucky.

The sad fact was that she did not make an entirely satisfactory pet but I was to grow quite fond of her simply because when you are six or seven years old there is an understanding between you and most of the animal kingdom and although you might infinitely prefer a cocker spaniel as a household pet you can make do with a goldfish if the situation dictates it. We had a rather unfriendly cat at that time called Micky and my father was still negotiating with my mother regarding dog ownership which I felt he did rather better than me though he wasn't having much success. Once the Rhode Island Reds arrived it amounted to almost a surfeit of pets but only if the seven of them could be included of course. My friend Molly who could be relied upon to know most things I didn't know because she was several months older than me and her birth date actually placed her into the year above me at school, said they could not be included under any circumstances because hens were not pets. I pointed out that Clucky was most certainly a pet and I had almost been given her for that specific purpose. Molly said well in that case, Jonah, old Mr Bassant's pig could also count as a family pet and nobody in their right mind would want him on account of the smell. You would never be able to keep him inside the house no matter how much you might want to.

The best thing about the hens was definitely the supply of fresh eggs and even Clucky joined in and did her bit now and again. As time went on Cecil Rhodes became more and more self-important and more unpleasantly aggressive and most especially when he became father to a clutch of fluffy yellow chicks, four or which eventually added to his harem. There had been several rooster chicks in the bunch and they were just as sweetly loveable as their sisters but overnight they disappeared and I was told they had gone to live on a farm owned by Lord Darnley near Cobham village. No matter how loveable the group had been when first hatched though, once they grew out of their fluffy, downy infancy, both Molly and I lost interest in them.

The worst thing about the whole poultry project was the fact that from time to time as had been predicted, a hen that had been pecking corn happily amongst its sisters and aunts one day would somehow find itself served up as a special Sunday dinner. Well it didn't quite happen like that because there would generally be a degree of discussion between my parents regarding what I could only view as the wilful murder of an inoffensive member of our extended family. My mother would invariably justify it by pointing out that the victim had not been such a reliable layer lately as if the bird had almost brought it upon herself.

My father would be sent out into the yard after tea to Wring its Neck as fast as possible and meanwhile I observed him from the kitchen window as he approached the coop that had once been our Anderson Shelter. It must have been the increased determination in his stride that alarmed the hens because they seemed to foresee what was about to happen and a shiver of apprehension would pass amongst them. Their flapping and squawking would grow a little louder and more urgent and Cecil might courageously attack the lower legs encased in scruffy wellington boots that approached. Within the kitchen I held my breath and tried to curb the tears as I contemplated the injustice of the slaughter that was about to take place telling myself that when I grew up and gained status and power no hen of mine would ever meet such a fate. I would only ever order poultry for cooking from the butcher in Dover Road just as we had indeed done ourselves before we became back street chicken farmers.

By next day the murdered fowl would be plucked and de-gutted and hung above the kitchen sink ready for Sunday roasting. And by Sunday when roasted potatoes, parsnips and carrots had been added and a bread sauce made by my father on the oven top, I would have recovered enough to tentatively eat a little of the white breast meat along with my aunts and cousins and whoever else might be sharing the meal.

At times like this my mother would preside over the vegetables proudly, pretending to be a competent cook and my father would carve the bird listening to her telling the room that there was a lot to be said for owning hens and it wasn't just the reliability of an egg for breakfast whenever you fancied one. In fact that wasn't quite true because in recent months she had decided that the majority of the eggs should be sold to my father's foreman from Bevan's Cement Works who was willing to pay a very good price as they were freshly laid. This was because he had a family of four children – two slightly hysterical girls called Brenda and Sylvia and two foster children, boys called Kevin and David who replaced a son dead at three from Leukemia. Such a family needed the input of freshly laid eggs in an age of austerity when their regularity was hard to come by.

I was charged with the weekly delivery and carried them carefully wrapped in newspaper and placed in a hessian bag to their house in Vale Road. It was a house that befitted a Bevans foreman, one I greatly admired and for a time desired to live in myself, Edwardian with a small front garden and a narrow entrance hall. A few years later when after my father's death I became familiar with the more upmarket houses in Darnley Road I was shocked that I had ever hankered after such a place but at eight it was my dream home and the inhabitants were very nearly my dream family. It wasn't that I modelled myself on either of the girls but the fact that they put a tablecloth on their table at teatime rather than sheets of newspaper was impressive and I couldn't help noting that their jam was not served directly from the jar it came in, but was put into a little glass bowl instead and you helped yourself with a spoon. When I told Molly about this she said they must be middle class and most likely had packets of real toilet paper in their lavatory, scratchy white stuff called Bronco. We were of course quite lower class and generally used newspaper torn into wipe-size pieces.

Over time we were to eat a number of our Reliable Layers and so I slowly became accustomed to the fact that murder lurked in our backyard and very possibly in other corners of York Road also. It did not go unnoticed that a number of neighbours kept rabbits and my cousin Harold jeered at me when I suggested they did so because they loved them. From my own point of view the ownership of rabbits would have been a great improvement on hens even if there was a vague intention to turn them into stews and pies at some stage. I might even have become accustomed to devouring the flesh of something I had cuddled to my breast and loved unconditionally, wept over and named because it had to be admitted that after a slow start I generally did my bit with regard to the consumption of the hens. I could only assume that over time my compassion became jaundiced and I realized that life was not always fair, especially where animals were concerned. And the shocking habit I knew to be not merely confined to animals because at school Mr Clarke had discussed cannibalism with us and told us that the taste of human flesh was said to resemble lamb a little. There had been sharp intakes of breath among the girls in the class when this was revealed whilst the boys nudged each other in excitement and sat up straighter.

When it was Clucky's turn to be eaten, sadly I had to draw a line because as an animal lover it was necessary to show the world that I had standards and it simply wasn't fair by any stretch of the imagination surely to expect children to eat their pets? My mother did a poor job of convincing me that it wasn't Clucky in the oven sizzling away, that in fact she had been sent to that lovely farm at Cobham to live out her days alongside her male relatives.

As I tearfully related the details of the hen's demise to Molly, hanging over the gate on Sunday afternoon whilst two aunts and my grandmother tucked into my pet hen, she said well it had been on the cards for a long time. In her experience that was the way of the world and just imagine being the owner of the pig, Jonah, because eventually he would meet the same fate and would take much longer to polish off. You could find yourself eating bacon rashers for weeks. You couldn't argue with that.

Of Canaries & Coalmines

Writing about Wombwell Hall invariably stirs up an assembly of fond memories. Safe to say that we past pupils may be quite different as far as our lives have developed but we are in total accord when it comes to the astonishing level of affection we still hold for the school. The very walls of the place, though existing now only in the mind's eye, have so willingly become wrapped around each one of us, offering a surfeit of comfort. And across the intervening decades our fervid response to our time there doesn't just relate to the grand old building but extends to many of the staff members including some of the most unlikely candidates.

In my own case there were probably more teachers I disliked or I was at least wary of than those I liked and I don't imagine that any of them would recall me with any degree of affection. However, my love affair with the place itself has ensured that I have kept every one of the eight school reports that document my academic progress between Christmas Term, 1953 and Spring Term, 1956. It's clear that the Hall had a similar effect upon its staff because not only did the majority of those noting my lack of scholarly headway remain in the job throughout the years I attended, many of them were still there ten years later.

Miss D Fuller was headmistress during my time and it's possible she was a Dorothy or a Deborah with friends who were not intimidated by her and called her Dot or Deb when they met up in the village pub for Sunday morning drinks. She seemed to me to be a tall, angular woman, slightly hunched, with a wardrobe full of tweed suits which she wore with striped blouses and occasionally men's ties and I kept as far away from her as possible. I was only sent to Report Myself to her on a handful of occasions, usually as a result of conflict with other girls, but on the odd occasion for uniform breaches.

During my first term Form G1 appears to have had two supervising Teachers, Miss S Smith who I now know to have been a Stella and who I remember well, and Miss M Cox who I have no memory of at all. I see now that my English teacher for the first three terms was someone with the initials MMH who never gave me a mark higher than B but said that at times my work showed thought and originality and that I should continue to apply myself. She may well have been the person that Miss S Smith got quite excited about, telling us we were indeed fortunate girls to be taught English by someone with a Master's Degree, a most exceptional academic achievement. She had then gazed around the room waiting for us to gasp in astonishment but with the exception of Valerie Goldsack who was prone to gasping at almost anything, we looked at each other in bewilderment and confusion. What on earth was a Master's Degree?

Furthermore MMH might in fact have been the very person who, lacking a considerable amount of insight and empathy suddenly and completely out of the blue stopped short in the middle of an explanation of the finer details of the plot of Prester John to stridently enquire if anything was worrying me. Not having the vaguest understanding of what she might be referring to I simply shook my head and so she said in that case perhaps I would like to stop staring out of the window and come to sit in the front row where my attention might become more engaged. What's more, once seated comfortably I might also like to explain to the class how Buchan had linked the Zulu uprising of 1910 to the medieval legend. As I did not want to do either of those things I said nothing at all but wondered why it was I was being seen as inattentive in the first place. Many years later it occurred to me that some of the ongoing distraction problems I had throughout my school years might have been due to the fact that I suffered from undiagnosed Temporal Lobe Epilepsy. On the other hand I might simply be giving myself an excuse as I was still most definitely more of an Enid Blyton aficionado than anything else. Prester John I suspect may simply have been too difficult a work to engage me at that time no matter how brilliantly it was being taught by this woman who possibly had a Master's Degree, whatever that eventually turned out to be.

During my first year a Miss SMH presided over Arithmetic, awarding me three lots of C- and noting that I found the subject difficult, was a slow worker and finally that I had a great deal of work to do before any kind of standard could be reached. She wasn't wrong and when we gave up the subject by Spring 1955 in favour of Accounts, although she was moved to say that I seemed to be making an effort and gave me an unadorned C, it is my firm belief that she was mistaken and in any event she was being extremely generous. For the duration of my Wombwell Hall years anything to do with figures continued to elude me and if I am completely honest nothing much has changed since.

Miss Springate who taught Geography was our 1SC Form teacher for two terms and I well recall clashing with her regularly and at times speaking to her quite rudely. My failure to get on with her is reflected in one documented examination result where I came twenty second in a class of twenty three. I'm still quite surprised by this result because I don't remember disliking her subject to that extent. Some of the topics had been moderately interesting and particularly so when we examined the history of coal mining in Kent, an industry that existed in our midst but was almost invisible. Miss Springate was able to inform us that in fact an open cast mine as close by as the environs of Cobham had reliably produced a quantity of useable coal which had actually been used by Lord Darnley to heat Cobham Hall. Two further drifts had recently been dug into the hillside and at one point the mine was thriving and producing 80 tons weekly. For some reason I found the idea of mining in Kent quite fascinating and even asked questions which was not like me and seemed to unnerve her. Were canaries taken into the Cobham drift just as they were in South Wales and in the North for instance? Were they found to be useful? I had recently read *How Green Was My Valley* and even researched something of the author Richard Llewellyn and was captivated by the possibility of all the drama that mining seemed to offer the working classes and disappointed to find the book's creator had been born in an outer London suburb.

Miss Springate did not seem to know a great deal about the canaries except that they were invaluable for detecting toxic gases so she moved quickly on to the village of Aylesham, not so very far from where we now sat, she said, and built in the 1920s specifically to house Kentish coal miners. Originally 20,000 residents had been expected but the building had turned out to be slower than expected. It was still, apparently, a work in progress. It was at that point that Valerie Goldsack said she knew a little about the village herself because an Uncle of hers was actually living there on a temporary basis as a mining consultant. He most definitely did not own or need to own a canary she hastened to assure us and then went on to explain about Test Bores and Failed Sinkings, further exhibiting her somewhat precocious knowledge. Miss Springate nodded approvingly.

Miss E Norman was our Form teacher for three terms and she taught several science subjects and might have been an Elizabeth or an Emily. She was fascinated by the sheep of the Romney Marsh and appeared astonished when we admitted to knowing very little about them because after all they were virtually on our doorstep so our lack of knowledge was abysmal. More importantly they were famous throughout the world. Why didn't we take the pride in them we should? We looked at each other helplessly and a few of us, like Valerie and those who sought to emulate her, might even have felt apologetic. Miss Norman had a habit of being surprisingly astonished by various aspects of our lives. On one occasion she was quite incredulous because only a handful of her form class had hot running water at home and they were the girls whose families were fortunate enough to have been recently moved into newly completed homes on housing estates.

When she recovered enough, she asked us what on earth we did when we needed to access hot water then? Anne Cogger, a quiet girl, said, somewhat aggressively for her, 'We fill a kettle up with cold water and boil it of course!' When Miss Norman looked as if she might have to sit down before she fainted, she added 'What else would we be likely to do?' The very nearly speechless science teacher looked about her and asked in a smaller voice, 'How many of you have to boil a kettle on each occasion you need hot water?' As a cautious plethora of hands began to rise she returned to fiddling with the Bunsen burners on the benches at the front of the room. I did not allow my own hand to rise though it was itching to do so because at the time I was engaged in a fantasy of mythological proportions about a substitute family living in a delightful thatched cottage close to the very centre of Cobham village which unlikely though it seemed sported every modern convenience available.

English was always my favourite subject and Miss K (Kate? Kathleen?) Smith was my favourite teacher despite her habit of only once giving me a mark above B- and repeatedly littering my reports with phrases like 'examination result very disappointing'… 'at times can produce good work' … 'capable of much better. … 'should spend less time daydreaming about the future.' Despite these comments she gave me time whenever I seemed to need it and suggested places where I might send short stories for publication. She became for me the font of all knowledge and when I had her complete attention I was in the habit of asking her opinion on all manner of issues that had little to do with the study of the English language. What was her opinion with regard to the use of canaries in Kentish coal mines? Why was the wearing of peep-toe shoes such an abomination? Her evasive replies did little to reduce my devotion to her. When she revealed to Miss S Smith my secret ambition to become a famous actress I was mortified but eventually was able to forgive her because it was difficult to hate her for too long and in any case we all knew that Miss S Smith and she were very close friends. So close that some girls, more sophisticated and worldly than me, sniggered knowingly when their friendship was mentioned. I had absolutely no idea what the suppressed mirth was all about and despite being thrown abruptly headlong into knowledge of sex and sin within a very short time of leaving the safety of school, it was a long time before I actually gave any real thought to the subject of same-sex relationships.

Some years later I was thrilled, though also startled and embarrassed, to come across the rather wonderful Miss Katie/Kathleen Smith holding court one Saturday evening in The Gateways Club in Kings Road, Chelsea. I had been taken there by a man I was obsessively in love with who thought I needed to broaden my horizons with regard to all matters sexual and what better place to start? She had definitely gained weight but her voice and bearing were unmistakable. She sat half astride a barstool in exactly the same way she had on a number of occasions sat beside me in the library at Wombwell Hall, advising me how to improve my writing, the wisdom of certain types of footwear and whether or not canaries had a special place in the hearts of Kentish miners.

She was wearing a look-alike tweed jacket to that which I remembered from 1955 and she had clearly had more than one gin and tonic but was by no means intoxicated. Had I been capable of doing so I might have engaged her in conversation but I did not take that option simply because I could not on the spur of the moment think of a convincing reason as to why I should be in what was described back then rather coyly as a Girls'Club. It did not occur to me that she might well have the same problem of course because she was Miss K Smith, and thus still neared perfection as a human being.

Years later, courtesy of other ex-Wombwell Hall students, I learned that she and her good friend Miss S Smith had shared a house together. I also learned that she was not everyone's favourite which came as a surprise to me. How could that possibly be so?

Fantails & Finches on Silk

Child labour is often associated with Victorian Britain and something somewhat mysteriously called Dark Satanic Mills that for years I thought were a form of windmill. As mills in my experience were always eye-catchingly attractive, I was at a loss to understand how anyone could possibly describe them as Satanic. This was clearly because I did not move very far from the riverside towns of industrial Kent where the darker variety were definitely absent. We were reassured that the evils of child labour had been eradicated by the great reforms that followed on the heels of the industrial age and in primary schools a great deal of emphasis was placed upon books like *The Water Babies*. Tom's misfortunes were discussed in depth at St Botolph's and it was constantly reiterated how fortunate we were to be born in the middle years of the enlightened twentieth century but in actual fact nothing is ever quite as it seems. My mother and her many siblings living in Maxim Road, Crayford in the earlier years of the new century and attending the local Roman Catholic school did so only from time to time because all too often they were needed for seasonal work to bulk out the family income. There was no question that paid employment came before the perils of child exploitation.

Maxim Road still exists though the cramped terraced housing has changed markedly and the Constant's two bedroomed rented cottage, so inadequate for thirteen lively children, can no longer be found. Old Nan always observed that despite its shortcomings it had been a Bleeding Sight Better than the farm cottage at Hextable where the oldest had been born and which had boasted a single sleeping area. Going up in the world always depends on how far down in it you were in the first place. Aunt Mag told her own four children that they were fortunate compared to the Constant sisters. The house in Iron Mill Lane on the estate built in the 1920s for Vickers' workers with its own garden, front and back to play in was almost luxurious. Living in Maxim Road, she said, had meant often playing on the Heath at Old Bexley and having to take the youngest ones along with you, rain or shine and staying there all day long or risking a clout around the ear for coming back early. Life had not been perfect and there hadn't been as much time for play as they would have liked but they didn't complain about their lot and overall they had been happy. Happiness seems to depend upon the level of misery it might replace.

The residents of Maxim Road did not realise that their road was named after Hiram Maxim, an American émigré who had abandoned his original wife and family and run off with Sarah his secretary. Not an unusual story of course but likely in those days to raise eyebrows in the district. Before long, however, Hiram had redeemed himself with the invention of curling tongs for hair and efficient mouse traps and it was even rumoured he had been a contender for invention of the electric light bulb. What brought him most renown though, and caused the enormous admiration of his brother Hudson who hurried from America to bathe in reflected glory, was becoming responsible for the Maxim Gun. This killing device had been updated and improved by 1912 when Vickers proudly presented it to the world where it remained in service until 1968. No wonder Hiram had his very own specifically-named local road.

When they weren't working the Constant girls were allowed to roam local streets, amusing themselves by knocking on doors and running away, swinging from lampposts and if they could find a length of rope, becoming totally occupied with skipping games. However, by the time each of them reached the age of twelve their mother who had never had a day's education in her life and felt that too much school attendance was of little advantage in life, applied for and was granted permanent exemptions. These were granted without comment, freeing each girl to enter a local factory and work not more than eight hours daily. Vickers was the factory of choice, the local populace being exceedingly proud of the place.

Back then children were rarely asked what they wanted to do when they grew up and if my mother had been asked she would have said, if she had been aware of the term, that the work of a textile artist greatly appealed to her. She would have liked to hand paint silk scarves and shawls with fantails and finches. There was little chance of this career choice ever presenting itself, however, and in effect each young Constant had worked on a part time basis before and after school for years at various times selling newspapers, as occasional milk girls, street hawkers, errand runners and frequently as artificial flower makers. The latter was popular because it could be done at home until late into the evening and from my mother's point of view the artistry and creativity took her a step closer to those greatly coveted fantails and finches. An investigation into child labour in London in the early 1900s found that a quarter of all children between five and thirteen had paid jobs of one kind or another but at twelve it was generally accepted that a child was old enough and responsible enough to take on regular employment.

Although I was suspicious of the authenticity of some of these stories of the generation that preceded my own they did much to convince me that by 1940 when I was born the British child was a great deal better off than those who immediately preceded them. There had clearly been far less time for fun for those of my mother's generation but by 1950 I don't recall ever being stopped from play in order to help with household tasks and there was never any suggestion that I should take a job before or after school. At times I was even asked what I wanted to do when I grew up and encouraged to mention working in an office. The working class child was at last definitely recognized as such which was a step forward because the State had treated Edwardian children much the same as adults and they were seen as legally responsible for their own behaviour from a very young age, but by the 1940s life had changed dramatically. Some of the local teenage boys might well have regretted the loss of the degree of independence that was previously offered them and the surprisingly adult privileges that went alongside such as the right to smoke, drink and even to gamble. Restrictions with regard to visiting pubs suddenly became the vogue and schoolchildren were no longer offered sugary gin spoons in public bars to keep them quiet. By my time lemonade and packets of crisps had been ushered in and we were placed firmly outside the pub doorways.

In fact this new attitude had been developing well before the First World War when the Children's Charter was established. It had introduced juvenile courts and decided that all under the age of fourteen should henceforth be seen as children. It then became illegal to sell children alcohol and tobacco but this was never enforced to any extent and fifty years later in Northfleet my grandmother could safely send me to the off-license happy in the knowledge that I would come back with a jug of beer. Some things were slower to change than others though, and when she was asked my mother admitted that the dream of hand-painting birds on backgrounds of silk remained with her long after she had left childhood behind.

Ultra-Short & Shaped

In 1951 the girls in their last year at St Botolph's began to opt for a hair style called Short & Shaped which the rest of us still burdened with plaits, bunches and ringlets thought enviably boyish. Wendy Selves and Jennifer Berryman both elaborately ringleted were decidedly more envious than the rest of us on account of regularly suffering the uncomfortable reality of curling rags which even my mother said was something you didn't adjust to easily. She didn't quite put it like that but I knew exactly what she meant because I had experienced the pain and horror of curling rags once or twice on the eve of the weddings of older cousins when it was important that I looked my best. Sleeping with them in situ on a regular basis was not something I was all that keen to try. Jennifer Berryman's grandmother said that it took her a full half hour to prepare the ragged-up hair each night and she said it proudly adding that she didn't mind because hair was a woman's Crowning Glory. Jennifer herself didn't say whether she minded or not. Wendy Selves said that her own hair had a natural curl in it and as a result her ringlets were not nearly as difficult to effect and maintain. Her best friend Jean Taylor said when Wendy was out of earshot that it was a lie and Wendy's hair was as straight as her own.

Molly from number 31 went to Northfleet Secondary Modern a whole year before me because of a well-timed birthday and during the week before she was due to start she joined the trickle of schoolgirls waiting for the attentions of Miss Joyce at Bareham's in Northfleet High Street clutching a two shilling piece in her hand. I was greatly impressed later that day, very much admiring of her newly-styled hair which was the shortest and most shaped Bareham's could deliver. Later my mother said it looked altogether too boyish for her liking and she was surprised that Miss Joyce would do such a thing to a child who didn't know any better. But Molly did seem to know better and was delighted with her new style and her own mother said as long as she was happy that was the main thing as she was the one who was going to live with it. Predictably my mother sniffed several times and said not for the first time that some people had no idea as to how to bring up kiddies. All in all it didn't seem the right time to campaign for the restyling of my own hair. In any case she had already reminded me several times that the recent Bareham's price rise for children from one and sixpence to two shillings was Daylight Robbery especially since Beryl's in Dover Road were still holding their prices down.

By the time Molly had been at the Secondary Modern for a month her own Ultra-Short & Shaped had grown enough for it to be cautiously admired even by some of the staff and she was told she had a beautifully shaped head that lent itself admirably to modern styles. The boost to her confidence was enormous and she could quite see why my primary aim in life became to sport a similar style especially when the main female contenders in St Botolph's Eleven Plus exam that year began to follow the example she had set. One by one Jacqueline Haskell,

Brenda Head, Pearl Banfield and Jean Taylor made visits to Bareham's or Beryl's after school and emerged with Ultra-Short & Shaped heads. They had mothers who were either aware of how important it was to be as similar as possible to every other girl of like age or, as I was firmly told, had money to burn. I knew we didn't have money to burn even though my father was not due to die from Acute Hepatitis until December and that was some months into the future. The other thing I knew without question was that there was not much point in appealing to him because unless I campaigned for books or trips of an edifying nature such as a Saturday afternoon visit to Rochester Castle, he wasn't ever much help to me. My cousin Pat who was a year my senior and whose father had already died at the end of the war by falling off a balcony in Italy in an inebriated state, frequently pointed out that fathers were not worth all the trouble they caused and she was very glad she didn't have one. Then I felt obliged to argue with her although I did so half-heartedly being quite aware that my own was not altogether ideal due to his ongoing obsession with both education and Fancy Women. These fixations caused both the primary females in his life, namely my mother and myself, to view him with some misgivings.

As far as hairstyles were concerned in any case Pat and I had very different ideas as to what was worthy of admiration as since the age of eight her own straight blonde tresses had been regularly subjected to what Aunt Martha, her mother said was a Wella Cold Wave. This meant that Pat's head sported a halo of tight curls for several months before it grew a little, became frizzy and not nearly as attractive and the whole cycle was repeated.

According to most of my aunts this attention to Pat's hair cost a fortune and definitely indicated that she was Spoilt Rotten. My mother said it was only affordable because the positive outcome of the unfortunate death of Uncle Paddy had been a War Pension which meant luxuries were common in their household. She did not of course say this directly to Aunt Martha. Other luxuries Pat had were hand-knitted silk boleros edged with angora and the regular home delivery of the Dandy and Beano comics. Apparently the home delivery confirmed that Aunt Martha had more money than sense. I was definitely envious of Pat a lot of the time but not because of the Wella Cold Waves and only marginally because of the angora-edged boleros. The home delivery of the comics definitely caused me some resentment because although my father was all in favour of reading matter, comics were not included.

When my occasional friend Margaret Snelling arrived at our house one Saturday afternoon to show off her new bike and her new Short & Shaped hair I was at a very low ebb and beginning to feel extremely infantile compared with my peers. Having plaits that when unplaited became a mane of hair that almost reached my waist was no longer the source of any degree of pride no matter how often people mentioned Crowning Glories. When I burst into tears after Margaret had gone home my mother said there was no use crying like a baby simply because I didn't have a bike and refused to believe me when I said that I didn't want a bike, all I wanted was to have my hair cut. My father tentatively suggested that surely it wouldn't be the end of the world for me to have a bike if I should actually make him proud by passing the Eleven Plus. But my mother looked very doubtful and said she didn't think I really had what it would take to become a Grammar School girl. He snorted a bit and told her that in his opinion I was as Bright as a Button and that The Grammar should be glad to have me. My own opinion was that what I wanted most in life was not a bike but Short & Shaped hair and to go to The Secondary Modern with Molly. But my opinion was not sought.

Over the next few days my father talked a lot about me being able to cycle to school and saving on bus fares and dropping into The Rainbow Stores to talk about time payment with them. My mother continued to express doubts and said a bike was an expense they could well do without and in case he hadn't noticed she was still saving up for a bird in a cage like Grace Bennet's because years ago she had loved the poor Linnet and now regretted giving it its freedom. She might go in for a budgie this time. She fancied a blue and yellow one because they were said to be good talkers.

The Rainbow Stores was opened in Stone Street in 1921 by Arthur Ernest Barnes who later branched out into radios and television sets and provided an excellent after sales service. Later still you could buy almost anything at The Rainbow and as Hire Purchase was becoming extremely popular and the selection of household goods impressive the business went from strength to strength. At the time of which I speak, however, I was much more interested in a Short & Shaped haircut than anything else although Molly said that was just silly and I should definitely accept the idea of a bike if one was being offered. Both the haircut and the proposed caged bird being saved up for could wait for a more auspicious moment. But of course I didn't see it quite that way. It was all very well for her with her Short & Shaped hair firmly in place and the regular upkeep of it now accepted.

Eventually I was allowed to have my Crowning Glory cut to just above my shoulders and even my grandmother shook her head and told my mother she hoped she wouldn't regret it because it was hair that helped to make a girl beautiful and some needed more help than others. My new semi-short hair was tied with ribbons into unattractive bunches and I did not feel that much progress had been made toward the modern world and of course hated them. In the interim my father announced that he had come to an arrangement with The Rainbow and if I passed the Eleven Plus I would definitely be getting a bike. He began to give me tests in arithmetic and the capitals of countries on Sunday afternoons which was a horrifying development, well at least the arithmetic was.

Despite the extra coaching my mother was proved right and I was not destined to become an exam success and so did not become the owner of a bike. I felt she took some degree of pleasure in telling me that I had broken my father's heart. Back in those days parents were less indulgent than they are now and actually meant what they said. My cycling future had depended one hundred per cent upon academic success. However, this was not as traumatic to me as it might have been had I been born fifty years into the future and therefore of necessity possessed of a more fragile psyche.

It was not until after my father's sudden death that I actually found myself in Beryl's of Dover Road with two shillings in my pocket because they had now matched Bareham's prices, having been instructed to have something done about the length of my hair that now hung untidily about my shoulders, still too short to properly plait. Controlling my excitement I told my mother that I would definitely make sure I came back with it much shorter and much tidier. She, being still distracted by the recent bereavement, barely looked up from the afternoon tea session she was sharing with Mrs Bennett from Buckingham Road. Half nodding she went back to the discussion on the shock a sudden death brings with it and how she was in a way relieved with regard to my exam failure though my poor father had set his heart on The Grammar. The problem was that I definitely favoured her side of the family rather than his. Her family had never been good at passing tests. It was in the blood and there wasn't much that could be done about it. And apart from all that there was the bus journey back and forth each day to be considered and the fares were not cheap were they? Not to mention the uniform, I mean the breath was nearly knocked out of her when she saw the cost of it. Mrs Bennett nodded in agreement and said her Joan was exactly the same when it came to passing tests and anyway there had been no question of her ever being allowed to go to The Grammar on account of her tendency towards travel sickness.

Beryl of Dover Road settled me into the freshly adjusted chair and said she supposed I wanted Short & Shaped like all the other local girls. It had been all the rage for nearly a year and certainly had kept her busy. I told her Yes, I wanted it as Short & Shaped as possible – Ultra-Short & Ultra-Shaped and as thoroughly modern as she could make it. So that is what she did. On the way home I felt distinctly nervous but elated and strangely light without my thick hair. I had prickly armpits but I admired my thoroughly modern self in every shop window. New bikes and going to The Grammar might be all very well for some but Short & Shaped was more my cup of tea!

Cups of tea were still being consumed at number 28 and Mrs Bennett observed that my hair was certainly very short but now much tidier. My mother absently agreed with her and then said that I looked more grown up somehow. Well with my father gone I would need to grow up a bit and take on more responsibility, perhaps look after my brother more she added. Mrs Bennett said you could never tell what bereavement might do to a child but at eleven it was probably time I grew up a bit. Then they began to talk more about budgies, blue and yellow ones that were reliable talkers.

Weddings & Woodpigeons

Old Nan said you could save a lot of money where weddings were concerned if you didn't have fanciful ideas leading to items like chicken salads. There was plenty of free food to be had if you only took the trouble to look for it. For somebody who had rarely been known to cook and whose dietary highlights revolved around fish and chips on Fridays and whelks on Sundays she sometimes came out with some very strange comments concerning food. Flo, engaged to my cousin Leslie and at the time planning her wedding breakfast, pretended she hadn't heard.

My grandmother looked annoyed which was never a good sign and spoke louder. She said that chicken was very dear and a tomfool idea if ever she'd heard one and nobody had starved back in 1930 not if they could be bothered to get off their fat arses and go out over to Crayford Marshes or them Cliffe marshes and the woods out wide of Gravesend where there were rabbits and woodpigeons aplenty. Aunt Mag, who Flo had recently started addressing as Mum in a slightly self-conscious way, said that it was never a good idea to go out with a gun when it was foggy though because that's how next door's Raymond had managed to get himself shot in the arm and very nearly killed. We all knew of course that he had come nowhere close to being killed but nobody was inclined to argue.

Flo was saying that it would be nice to have a fruit trifle made with proper sherry and perhaps some Libby's or even ice cream and what did Mum think. But before my aunt could think anything at all, my grandmother had got to her feet and with the aid of a knitting needle pointed our forcibly that a fruit trifle was another tomfool idea because how could you make one big enough for forty or fifty people. Flo snapped that it didn't have to be one trifle because it could be three or even four. So she sat down again saying that Iced Fancies ordered from the self-same place as made the wedding cake had been good enough for young Margaret and Jack and were going to be good enough for young Harold too before That Cow Joan had thrown him over. There was a silence then because nobody liked talking about Joan and the jilting. My cousin Pat had told me that she certainly hoped Joan had thought long and hard before dumping Harold because after all she was twenty-eight and definitely well and truly On the Shelf. In fact it wouldn't be an exaggeration to say our Harold had probably been her Last Chance. In any case, she added, it wasn't as if he was much of a Looker but then at twenty-eight Joan could hardly afford to be too fussy. I didn't altogether agree with her because to me Young Harold seemed definitely better looking than his recently betrothed brother and at least he didn't have a stomach ulcer and still had all his own teeth if what he said was true.

Aunt Mag had been almost as distraught as her jilted first-born when That Cow Joan made her momentous decision to dump poor Harold three weeks before the wedding that had been booked at St Paulinus Church for more than six months. Old Nan said it was a Sign and the whole shebang had been doomed before it got off the ground and should always have been planned for St Mary of the Crays and she certainly hoped that the ring had been returned. She wouldn't put it past that Fast Floozy to try to get away with it. But that could not have been further from the truth and the only getting away had been Joan getting away from Harold. According to my mother, there had been one helluva barney and the ring had apparently been thrown across the room, landing in the very-nearly-dumped groom's plate of Saturday evening tripe and onions.

You could have knocked his doting mother down with a feather because Young Joan had never previously displayed such behaviour and she did wonder if it was all down to the time of the month – or even not the time of the month. At that thought she and my mother exchanged knowing glances. But when she had tried to intervene on Young Harold's behalf she had been told to keep her pointy nose well out of it because it was between him and Joan and nothing to do with any of his interfering family. The Linyards were altogether too interfering as far as Joan was concerned, always meddling and snooping and wanting to know everything not to mention spreading other people's private and personal business throughout the extended family so that in the end even the kiddies were aware of things they should never by rights be aware of.

Relaying all this to my mother the day that followed what they both agreed was a palaver if ever there was one, she could not emphasise enough what a shock it had all been and what a common, vulgar cow that Joan had turned out to be and her language had to be heard to be believed because things had been said that my aunt could never bring herself to repeat. However, she did bring herself to whisper them once my brother and I had removed ourselves to the scullery and my mother's sharp intake of breath confirmed the extent of the profanity. Harold was well shot of that Joan of that there was no doubt.

Once she knew the ring had been returned, well, retrieved really from the middle of her distraught grandson's supper plate, Old Nan ventured to comment that it was a pity about the new wedding suit made to measure by a tailor in Dartford. That, of course, had been another one of that Joan's tomfool ideas and a complete waste of money though it could probably be worn at his brother's forthcoming nuptials. The pale lemon satin bridesmaid's dresses with chiffon overskirts, also demanded by Joan and made by the woman in Horton Kirby, were another problem because chiffon might have been all very well for Joan but Flo had made it perfectly clear that she wasn't prepared to accept pale lemon or chiffon under any circumstances. Her own bridesmaids were to be clad in pink with definitely not a trace of chiffon. The three dresses hung like pale ghosts in Aunt Mag's wardrobe, swinging softly back and forth each time the door was opened. Whenever they were mentioned she said to just leave it and Flo would Come Round but Leslie the husband-to-be was not convinced. The dresses got mentioned frequently of course and with increasing anxiety by the two small cousins on our side of the family who had been destined to wear them. Little Susan even wondered if the four-year-old flower girl from Joan's side would come to claim the smallest one with a view to perhaps wearing it to a Christening. She did not do so though.

It became clearer than ever after the dumping of Harold that Flo, his younger brother's formerly more malleable fiancée, was becoming less flexible as the date of her own wedding approached despite the fact that she was beginning to address his mother as Mum with more and more confidence. When my grandmother unwisely again brought up the subject of putting woodpigeons on the wedding breakfast menu Flo turned on her firmly and said hell would freeze over before any wedding guest of hers would be forced to eat a bloody pigeon so drop the subject once and for all. And rather surprisingly that is precisely what Old Nan did, after muttering a bit about never having been spoken to like that before in her life and what was wrong with pigeons and there were some, especially toffs, who'd pay a fortune to lay their hands on them. At which of course, Flo said well the toffs were more than welcome to them and then softened the retort by buying the next round of drinks because it was a Saturday evening and this conversation took place in The Jolly Farmers an hour or so before my mother decided we should catch the next 480 bus back to Northfleet.

My brother, lingering in the doorway with two cousins and a packet of salt and vinegar crisps, said in his experience people often got woodpigeons muddled up with Stock Doves and he wasn't sure if the latter were altogether as edible. My mother said to button his lip and that chicken salad had now been quite decided upon. We both knew she was firmly taking this stand because Flo was well within earshot, standing at the end of the bar with two pound notes in her hand and an attitude of largesse about her.

We had rapidly developed a new respect for the woman who was shortly to marry our cousin Leslie even though it would be some time before Old Nan Constant would entirely forgive her for her steadfast attitude with regard to chicken salad and trifles made with sherry. Flo had very recently taken to distributing packets of Smith's Crisps to those family members too young to enter Licensed Premises and therefore congregating outside the pub which of course ensured her ongoing popularity with the young. Her insistence that her wedding was definitely to take place at the Holy Apostles Church in Swanley was a hurdle harder to manage by the family elders. As the day grew closer though even Aunt Mag now firmly established as Flo's Mum was beginning to accept the fact that as the girl grew up in Swanley it stood to reason that she would want to be married there and you had to allow for the other side of the family having some input into wedding arrangements. Predictably not everyone agreed with her and freshly married Margaret, now wed to Jack the owner of a smart red sports car, rather uncharacteristically commented that was the problem with both the Constants and the Linyards. They really did not understand the meaning of co-operation and teamwork.

But in fact she was not completely correct because by the time the wedding day grew closer Flo had as predicted Come Round at least with regard to the pale lemon bridesmaids dresses and had even found someone in her Swanley family belonging to a second cousin who was small enough to be the flower girl. What's more Young Harold did indeed wear the tailor-made suit at the event and looked very dapper indeed and was quite chipper even though he was still shell-shocked from the unexpected jilting and though a number of female relatives pressed him to provide a reason for what had actually happened he steadfastly refused to elucidate further.

In spite of her new-found flexibility Flo did not waver for a moment with regard to the wedding breakfast menu and was heard to say more than once after two or three Saturday evening Babychams that if anyone thought she was going to allow pigeons to be substituted for her proposed chicken salads they could think again and that Nan Constant could take a running jump and she would tell her so herself if need be. She did not do so of course and at the wedding everyone, including my grandmother complimented her on the excellent food. All in all it turned out to be a most successful event.

In particular the photographs were much better than average and definitely a step up from those taken at Margaret and Jack's wedding. This, Margaret maintained, was only because Our Lady of Assumption on The Hill at Northfleet always seemed to be in shadow. It was, she thought, a church that was better suited to funerals than to weddings. Flo of course was delighted because in her photographs not only was nobody wearing plastic ear-rings which she abhorred but perhaps more importantly everyone was smiling. Everyone except Young Harold, who stood morosely in his smart suit with shoulders hunched and a cigarette between his lips looking for all the world like Marlon Brando except of course taller and without a motorbike. Because he and I did not exactly get on well together as cousins go, after two forbidden glasses of orange juice laced with gin I asked him if he was missing Joan and if he still loved her. He stared over my shoulder fixing his eyes on the doorway at the very end of what the Jolly Farmers at that time called The Function Room. He said that Joan had meant everything to him and then he added that I should Piss Off. So I did.

No-one was to know of course that within a very short space of time Jilted Harold would meet the love of his life, Sylvia who came from Hemel Hempstead and, as Aunt Mag pointed out, differed from That Cow Joan in every way. When within a matter of months the two got married, Harold was able to once again wear the made-to-measure suit and Sylvia endeared herself to everyone by agreeing with both the Constants and the Linyards when they offered wedding advice. She was even heard to tell Old Nan that the idea of woodpigeons at the wedding breakfast sounded like a smashing idea. Flo told her she was making a rod for her own back by agreeing to the ideas of That Wicked Old Cow but Sylvia just laughed and when the great day dawned what was served was very similar to the menu that had been offered by Flo.

My brother, tucking into slices of white breast meat adorned with a single piece of lettuce said that although the idea of the woodpigeons had been interesting he was still unsure as to how easily they might be muddled up with Stock Doves. He was not at all convinced that the latter were edible. They might even be poisonous. He thought that Flo might very well agree with him.

Theft in Lord Darnley's Woods

For us Cobham Woods was never a place for quiet meanderings on spring evenings such as those described in volumes with titles like *Kent Walks* or in information leaflets for ramblers but always a special destination, much planned for in advance. There had to be a certain amount of pre-planning because a kettle had to be packed together with the oldest and most chipped cups, leaf tea, sugar, milk, sandwiches and biscuits and of course matches for igniting the camp fire. It had to be leaf tea because this was a time before even the most rudimentary tea bags. Sometimes if Molly was to come with us the cups would include the one that was kept at the back of the shelf for the aunt on my father's side who my mother said looked consumptive. The milk was never fresh but usually what was left in a can of sweetened condensed. As for the sandwiches, my mother was very fond of cheese with Branston's pickle or even Daddy's sauce when the pickle was running low. The biscuits were usually of the broken variety that I was regularly sent to Penney, Son & Parker on The Hill to buy on Friday afternoons because either the Trokes of Shepherd Street did not stock them or Peggy and Vic were not to know that broken was always our first option. I didn't mind too much because biscuits of any kind were a treat as far as I was concerned.

Occasionally the picnics took place more spontaneously as a weekend family outing but in springtime they were prearranged as more strategic exercises specifically for the purposes of stealing Lord Darnley's primroses. I doubt that Lord Darnley himself was aware of the thefts or if he was he chose to ignore the fact and to be quite honest I did not really understand that what we were doing amounted to theft. That's what happens when you grow up in a family where shoplifting was not discouraged and minor embezzlement and pilfering was accepted as the norm as long as you were not silly enough to get caught.

Garden Centres as we now know them did not seem to exist back then, or at least not for people like us. Vegetables and flowers were things you grew from seeds in little packets with colourful pictures on the front so that even if you were unsure of the word carrot or cabbage you knew what it was you were likely to end up with. You could buy them at the back of Rayner's in Northfleet High Street and sometimes even in Woolworths. Some people, more mysteriously, produced the plants they desired from cuttings donated or perhaps filched from the gardens of neighbours known for having Green Fingers. In any case it is unlikely that my mother would have easily sanctioned the idea of spending money on something as frivolous as flowers when they existed in abundance in nearby farmers' fields and gardens, on roadsides and of course in even further diversity in Lord Darnley's woods. Old Mrs Bassant whose cousin had once been in service at The Hall said that The Darnleys had taken less and less interest in the entire estate over the years which was understandable once the place had been overrun with evacuees and RAF officers from the Battle of Britain squadron for years and they must be sick to death of not being able to call their home their own any more. Even the family mausoleum had fallen into disrepair and deer and cattle were to be seen grazing around it because they had ceased to care enough about it.

The mausoleum was always the first place we visited, entering the strangely foreign-looking construction in silence, breathing softly and hardly daring to allow our shoes to reverberate, as if we were in church. When my father explained in a low voice that we must show respect because this was the final resting place of the Darnley dead I could feel my heart pounding in my chest so loudly that I was fearful that the souls of the dead might also hear it and leap out of their stone alcoves to remonstrate with me. Later, gathering kindling for the fire with my mother, she would tell me of the local man who had for a wager elected to be locked in the place overnight. He had entered with a shock of black hair which by morning had turned completely white and he could never be persuaded to speak of his experience. Even then this story sounded slightly implausible to me but nevertheless I repeated it to Molly at the first opportunity knowing that she could be relied upon to be interested albeit disbelieving.

We always attended to the serious business of the picnic before tackling the unearthing of primroses and the best part of that was the lighting of the fire and keeping my brother away from it because it was dangerous and he was too young to understand the dreadful consequences of being burned. My mother's own recollection of being left in charge of younger siblings in Maxim Road, Crayford in 1917 on the occasion of a fire breaking out was all too vivid and although she never quite revealed all the pertinent details as to how it happened and what the actual damage to life and limb had been, the trauma of the event was still evident on each occasion the possible dangers of fire were spoken of.

It wasn't too difficult to keep Bernard away from the flames because even before he could walk he was much more entranced by the antics of the woodland birdlife and on each visit over several years his attention was completely captivated by them. As he grew older and the picnics ceased upon the death of my father he frequently ruminated over the memory and maintained that he clearly recalled that his first sightings of quite uncommon avian types was in the woods at Cobham, birds that included the Hawfinch, Willow Tit, the Spring migrant, the Nightingale and on one occasion even a Goshawk. But the most exciting of all had been what he years later recognized to be the Night Jar, the master of disguise, a bird with an almost supernatural reputation said to be able to feed from milk stolen from unwary goats. There were limited numbers of goats in the area and to be completely honest the only one I had ever seen was in a library book called *Farm Life for City Children* which didn't even mention stolen milk but my brother's recollections in later years were vibrant if not exaggerated. At the time, while he was so occupied, sometimes not even demanding to be released from the confines of his push chair, the kettle was placed on the flames to boil and the cheese and pickle sandwiches were unwrapped and set out upon the verdant grassy area within view of the mausoleum. Mrs Bassant had told us that when The Hall was first built a landscape designer, a Mr Repton, had been hired at enormous cost to ensure that the family should have an undisturbed and sweeping view of their resting dead as they sat in the drawing room sipping gin and tonics. At the time of our picnics the undergrowth of decades ensured that view had completely vanished.

The initial campaign for stolen plants had emerged shortly after my father arrived home from his six-to-two shift one afternoon uncharacteristically late with squares of turf in the sidecar of the motor bike, carefully protected by newspaper but all the same causing my mother some annoyance. There was shortly to be a lawn installed adjacent to the old Anderson Shelter. A place for her to sit in the afternoon sun and perhaps read a newspaper he told her persuasively but she remained what she described as 'none too keen'. For me it was an exciting development because people in books had gardens, albeit rather more elaborate than our own was going to be. I knew ours would of necessity be modest but a proper garden all the same and a garden promised endless possibilities. To my father, carefully laying the intriguing squares of turf in the small space between our outdoor lavatory and the now largely disused shelter, it first and foremost meant a border of flowers and where better to start than with Lord Darnley's primroses? Old Mr Bassant commented that a border of carrots and cabbages would have been equally pleasing to him and that might well have been so because his eyes were known to light up at the thought and sight of vegetables. But as my mother morosely pointed out, we were currently dead set on flowers and my Aunt Mag, not known for love of growing things herself, commiserated and said that she blamed these ideas on the aftermath on the war and in time he might well go off the idea but of course he didn't. In fact that very next weekend found us engaging in our first foray of woodland robbery. Later my brother claimed he remembered it as the day he first saw the Hawfinch which was far more exciting than the squabbling sparrows and starlings in York Road, though again he may have been exaggerating.

Although at times I pretended to be half-hearted I was never completely uninterested in trips to the woods because entering a space where mature trees dominated was invariably energizing and the reason for being there did not seem to matter very much. Oak, Beech, Hornbeam and Sweet Chestnut could be relied upon to provide a canopy beneath which in imagination, assignations could take place and secrets might be divulged. Woods were places where Enid Blyton's characters habitually came face to face with dangerous criminals, explored long abandoned buildings, solved perplexing mysteries long before the local police force, and of course topped up their energy levels with cold tongue, ham sandwiches, jam tarts and lashings of ginger beer. Our own picnics were of the more humble variety but I was pleased because although the Five had access to the ginger beer I was so envious of, they missed out on the campfire necessary for kettle boiling.

Molly joined us when her mother said she could and was very keen to do so at Conker Time in late September or early October when the horse chestnuts lay in thick prickly carpets underfoot. Northfleet children were enthusiastic conker players back then and Alan Bardoe always said that to win a game you had to start with really hard conkers because they were the ones that would win. As they hardened with age he was in favour of keeping a selection of the biggest and best to use the following year. He called them Laggies because that's what his father said they were and was known to soak them in vinegar and paint them with clear nail varnish which his opponents said was definitely cheating. His twin, Colin, said all that was nonsense in any case and the way to ensure a win was to make sure that a clean and round hole had been bored through in the first place. Both Molly and I were of the opinion, with no basis of fact to back it up, that the Cobham conkers were the best in Kent.

We would have been astounded had we been able to look ahead to the turn of the century when the game was to be banned in many schools for fear of unnecessary injuries and that particularly caring parents would provide their offspring with goggles as a precaution. The fact that some schools would choose to forbid conkers completely for fear of causing anaphylactic shock in students prone to nut allergies would have been a completely outlandish idea. In the late 1940s nut allergies were something that also belonged in the oddly fanciful country of the future together with Asperger's Syndrome and Attention Deficit Disorder.

For my father, intent upon establishing a garden oasis in our York Road back yard, the visits to the woods simply meant the acquisition of free flowers, and we appropriated them with enthusiasm during the months of March and April until the borders of our tiny green space was strident with various shades of yellow. My mother was, overall, more fond of the stately rows of rhododendrons that emerged in spring and seemed to last for weeks into the summer, calling them Glorious. I disliked them for their lofty determination to be noticed and was glad when she seemed far too intimidated by their presence to carry blooms home with her. My favourite flower became the bluebell, growing alongside the primroses and delightfully easy to gather in armfuls for Molly and me as we pulled them from their beds with a savagery that ensured they would not re-emerge the following year.

Mrs Gunner, the vicar's wife, observing our plundered spoils shook her head disapprovingly and told us that no good could possibly come from stealing plant life from Lord Darnley's woods because it was called Vandalism. She added that in years to come we would realise the damage we had done, the kind of harm in fact that would kill off the woodland completely if we were not careful. Then we were offended knowing that she should have better directed these observations towards the adult thieves but saying to each other that it was none of her business and in any case there was no good reason why we should pay any heed to what she said. Of course none of us were to know then that by the year 2001 funding would be provided for the local Council to purchase the woods together with the mausoleum on the understanding that ownership would eventually pass to the National Trust to ensure that the 600 acres of natural beauty would be preserved. The general idea of caring for the environment was again something that belonged to the strangely unpredictable future. My father would have been astonished to know that with the dawn of environmental concern a total of ninety-five abandoned cars would be removed from the periphery of the woodland, the very space where we regularly left the motor bike and side car. Vehicular access therefore was to become severely restricted for the would-be primrose purloiners of the future.

The Fuse Box in the Coal Cupboard

Tess Leyton came back to Northfleet after an absence from the area of seven years and rented the Finches' old house just a few doors away from us. She brought with her a brand new husband called Bill, an impossibly handsome teenage son called Ramon, named for a cinema heart-throb of the nineteen thirties, and a small daughter called Junie. She was also proudly accompanied by a breeding pair of canaries because she was seriously contemplating going into the pet bird business there being money in it and what's more it didn't need a great deal of space. We had not quite decided upon the acquisition of the budgerigar called Ricky that we eventually owned for several years and so a canary was being earnestly considered because of the anticipated beauty of its song. My mother was confident she might learn a great deal from Tess Leyton. She seemed to have her head screwed on the right way and that was a fact.

Tess immediately renewed her acquaintance with us saying that she and my mother were Old Mates. Nellie, not accustomed to people seeking her friendship, was flattered by the attention though she said that back in 1944 they hadn't been particularly close and one of the reasons for that was that Tess had then lived in Shepherd Street. It might only have been a hop, skip and a jump away but wartime was wartime when all was said and done and Doodlebugs were known to be unpredictable. What's more back then Tess had been husbandless and considered somewhat Blousy and some locals like Grace Bennett had even referred to her as a Slummock and a fat cow which wasn't altogether congenial. But then Grace always had a sharp tongue and it didn't do to get on the wrong side of her. Then again Tess Leyton could never have been described as a small woman and was always loud and opinionated. Before painting her too black though there was the tragedy of her Little Nova, the previous small daughter, to be considered. That poor little mite had been lost following an accident involving boisterous play on top of an Anderson shelter which might never have happened if the shelter had been properly installed in the first place and not just thrown up half-baked.

Little Nova had been named for Nova Pilbeam, a well-known actress of the nineteen thirties. We wondered who Little Junie had been named for but it seemed rude to ask and Tess did not venture to tell us right away. What she did tell us, however, was that Little Junie was precious and that they had almost Lost her at birth, she was also delicate and Dr Outred was very keen indeed to keep a special eye on her. My mother seemed to debate as to whether or not to reveal that I was also delicate and decided not to for which I was grateful. Eventually we were to learn that Little Junie had been named in honour of June Allyson, an up and coming American actress that the rest of us had barely heard of. Tess was an avid film fan and went to the Majestic in Gravesend with her Bill every Saturday evening without fail. Occasionally when her Ramon was not available for watching Little Junie, she would come along to our house and share a bed with my brother until her parents returned.

Back in the Shepherd Street days of World War Two when Grace Bennett said there had been talk that Tess had at times been no better than she ought to have been, she was not a Leyton at all and I'm not even sure if I ever knew what her name once was but I did know that her original husband was called Ron and he had met with a nasty accident when his old push bike with the basket on the front collided with a 496 bus in the blackout. The basket had been piled high with purloined paper from Bowaters where he was doing essential war work because of his eyesight. Sad though the accident was my mother had never really taken to Ron and that might have had something to do with him not having received his Calling Up papers. She always found such situations challenging. Old Mrs Bassant said if his sight had been better he might have actually seen the bus and he should have been issued with proper cycling glasses in the first instance if the work was so essential.

With Ron now completely out of the picture, when Bill appeared on the scene with the return of Tess and her canaries, my mother found him much easier to take to in the early days of their acquaintance. However, even this scant regard was to diminish following my father's death and that unfortunate development was one hundred per cent due to the fuse box in the coal cupboard.

Each small dwelling in our York Road terrace, and also those similar that surrounded us, was blessed with the convenience of electric light and the necessary fuse box lived adjacent to the coal in the cupboard under the stairs. Before the dawn of electricity in the area lighting came in the form of gas lamps attached to the walls, supplemented at times with conveniently mobile paraffin lamps. I can't remember and perhaps I never actually knew when the gas lighting became totally obsolete, and when I was very small I clearly recall the wall lamps still being lit in my bedroom from time to time.

Both gas and electricity supplies were fed with coins into the mysterious slot meters that lived among our coats and scarves at the bottom of the steep narrow stairs leading to the floor above. Gas had been installed throughout the country at the turn of the twentieth century and by the 1920s there were more than seven million users with average families spending between one and two pounds per annum on the commodity. Our gas meter had a very Edwardian look about it, was only slightly threatening and was regularly and confidently fed with dull, dark pennies. For years I had been allowed to drag a chair underneath with a coin in my hand and, feeling important and grown up, operate the lever when the supply inconveniently expired during the roasting of the Sunday dinner. The copper coins dropping into the receptacle gave a satisfying clank which grew more muted as the meter filled. Even though its odour was disagreeable and the lighting of the rings of the stove in the corner of the scullery was exhilarating even to watch, in its entirety the miracle of gas was familiar. I knew that middle-aged women who lived on their Nerves or had husbands who Drank sometimes chose to end their lives by uncomfortably placing their heads in ovens, often without even a cushion to support them, but nevertheless I had few qualms regarding its danger. This was only because electricity was said to be much more perilous. It was certainly much more costly.

The spread of electricity had been slow to proliferate through English towns and villages, particularly so in unambiguously working class streets and terraces such as ours. When it did come to York Road the small and sleek, much more modern and important looking meter sitting alongside that of the gas company demanded one shilling pieces. This was to my mother's mind an eye-watering expense and therefore leaving lights on by accident when exiting the house was an offence that would not be forgotten for days and she was open mouthed in amazement when my newly engaged cousin Margaret announced that what she wanted more than anything as a wedding present was an electric bar heater. Quite apart from the infinitely lower cost of gas, in our house we came to feel that whatever its shortcomings, it was a much more convenient energy source. This feeling became ever more entrenched and this was largely because its delivery did not depend upon fuses of any kind. Fuses were what was categorically wrong with electricity although we had not quite realized this whilst my father was still alive. This only proves that what looms large and significant in anyone's life depends entirely on their current circumstances.

For instance Pearl Banfield from number six, once she started Going Steady with someone called Graham at the age of seventeen said that the local electricity supply was definitely the thing she found most abhorrent about living in York Road. What had previously been insufferable to her and where she had my total support, was the outside lavatory but now her engagement was looming her attitude had changed. This was because now that they were Serious, Graham was allowed to visit on Saturday evenings and sit with her in the front room. The humiliation of the lights suddenly going out and everyone rummaging in pockets and purses for a shilling piece was embarrassing in the extreme Pearl declared. It did not happen at Graham's house where electricity was delivered effortlessly followed by a monthly bill which his mother ensured was paid regularly. Pearl lived in fear of the extinguishing of the Saturday evening lights, just as she had once lived in fear of Graham needing to use the toilet.

My mother became equally preoccupied with possible interruptions to the supply and for her it was not the fact that there might be a paucity of one shilling pieces because she now took the precaution of having one or two at hand, but rather because a Fuse might need to be Mended and that was most definitely a man's job. After December 1951, with my father no longer present and my brother still much too young to be considered male enough for the job, we would of necessity remain without avant garde lighting until an Uncle or older cousin dropped by to visit. I never thought this was too much of a calamity as we still had the illumination of gas available to us but Nellie was distraught to be without the comfort of the wireless, unable to do the weekly ironing and as the years went by, unable to watch the twelve inch television set.

On a couple of occasions Mary Newberry who eventually replaced Old Mrs Bassant next door promised to send her Charlie in after work but obviously forgot all about it and had to be reminded twice because she was a silly cow if ever there was one – and even when he did turn up he said he needed the right kind of fuse wire and a special trip had to be made over to Woolworths next day.

All this caused a great deal of stress so once a friendship had been re-established with Tess Layton and innumerable afternoons had been spent with her drinking Mazawattee tea and dunking Nice biscuits, a tentative request was made that her Bill might come along and deal with the fuse problem. Tess said he would be only too pleased to help out because if there was one thing you could say about her Bill, it was that he was obliging. Everyone said so! He turned up as promised just after five o'clock, even armed with fuse wire and was delighted to find that we had stocked up and had several different thicknesses of wire wound efficiently around a card just waiting to be deployed. There was nothing worse, Bill said, than using the wrong wire because you didn't want to overload the circuit did you? And of course we didn't want to do that under any circumstances.

Bill Leyton most willingly, with very good grace, did mend the fuse and executed the task in just a few minutes, refusing a cup of tea and even saying that he was only too glad to be of assistance. So all would have been well had it not been for my mother, overcome with gratitude after several powerless days pressing a two shilling piece into his hand urging him to treat himself to a pint at The Prince Albert up the road. To be quite fair to Bill, he initially vehemently declined to avail himself of this unexpected pint and she, just as resolutely insisted that he should do so and so after a small tussle he pocketed the florin and thanked her very much.

This was undoubtedly a faux pas extraordinaire although I was seriously perplexed as to why at the time. My mother's indignation was extreme as she both rebuked herself for the folly of the request for help and berated the now long-gone recipient of the reward to all who would listen. My small brother and I were harangued over hours and asked what kind of man takes a couple of bob from a widowed neighbour? Did he really think she had money to throw away on the likes of him? Mending a fuse was a doddle after all for a man like him. It took the biscuit, it really did. Did he think she had money to burn? Would she be scrubbing her knuckles to the bone around at the Lovell's every Monday morning in all weathers if she could afford handouts for what rightly should have been a favour?

My grandmother and aunts were similarly addressed because when you considered the fact that he was happy to take her money, bold as brass in fact you had to ask yourself what decent man would lower himself like that. What about all the tea that lazy slummock of a wife of his could knock back? Not to mention the biscuits! Yet when you dropped by her place you'd find the milk would only ever be sterilized and the biscuits never ever Bourbon or Custard Creams.

When she told Grace Bennett the criticism which had now turned into a barrage of abuse, was of course strictly between the two of them but my mother was nearly blown off her feet when he actually put his hand out to take that couple of bob from her. Quick as a flash he was – couldn't wait to pocket it! She was never going to stoop to ask him again and next time she ran across Tess she would clean her something rotten. And Grace said well she herself had never taken to Tess Leyton and hadn't she always said that Blousy Cow and was not to be trusted. You only had to think back to the first husband and the stolen goods and then there was the pair of them always out on a Friday night gallivanting and those poor kiddies left to fend for themselves. Grace was only glad my mother had finally seen the light because she wouldn't be told would she?

Of course the matter of the pocketed florin was never brought up with Tess Leyton because if there was one thing that my mother lacked it was moral fortitude or what we would now refer to as backbone. Furthermore the next time the fuse needed attention, after almost a week without power, and no convenient visits from teenage cousins she did in fact ask for Bill Leyton's help once again. And once again she firmly pushed a two shilling piece in his direction, only this time with pursed lips and a raised chin. And once again after an initial refusal he pocketed it at which she bridled a little and folded her arms disapprovingly as she thanked him very much for his help in a voice that was imperceptibly too loud.

She was thus destined to continue to feel affronted but as far as was possible she spent less time drinking Mazawattee tea with Tess Leyton. It was around that time that the decision to buy Ricky the budgie was made and in any case the canary breeding idea came to nothing in the end – like all that Leyton woman's tomfool notions!

Not a Patch on Going Hopping

In the nineteen forties and fifties people didn't go on holidays nearly as much as they seem to nowadays. One good reason for several years was obviously the war but I'm not sure that people like us holidayed a great deal in the nineteen twenties or thirties either for that matter. Some in the community who were deemed by my mother to think themselves Better than us, Mrs Frost of Springhead Road for example, were determined to ignore the war and courageously set off in 1941 for their annual week in Broadstairs or Folkestone, often to visit relatives. In Mrs Frost's case it was the sister who conveniently ran a guest house in Hastings but on this occasion her plans were ill fated. The reason for this was we found as she breathlessly relayed the story to the curious customers in Hilda Simms' corner shop, that she had been targeted by a Dornier just overhead when she and her sister were about to step into Plummers. They were almost gunned down where they stood and would have surely perished if it hadn't been for a brave little Spitfire, rising up above the enemy plane and giving chase. Later her nephew told her that the Dornier had fallen into the sea and the Spitfire had done a double victory roll to cheers from the onlookers on the blustery seafront below. After that experience which grew ever more dramatic with each retelling, Mrs Frost paid more heed to the fact that we were a country at war and decided to put all thoughts of holidays on hold for the duration.

It was all very well for people like the Frosts, I was told, whose income was very well supplemented by the piano lessons given in the front room after school each day, but those of us further down the social scale could only contemplate such extras once the Holidays with Pay Act was passed in 1938 whether or not a war was on the horizon. Even then it benefited only those workers whose wage rates were fixed by Trade Boards and were thus awarded one week on full pay, no questions asked. This was seen as a great step forward. By 1948 a couple of our neighbours spoke of booking a week at Butlin's in Clacton. The Scutts family who lived at the top of Springhead Road quite close to The Leather Bottel had actually been there twice according to Barbara who was in my class at St Botolph's. However, Barbara was known to exaggerate. Rita Jenkins confidently told us that she was being taken to Butlins at a place called Skegness which was miles away and her mother was busy sewing her two new summer dresses. I began to seriously hanker after the undoubted glamour of a holiday camp!

The first such camp was opened by John Fletcher Dodd at Caister-on-sea in 1906 and called, unimaginatively, Caisters. Nobody I knew ever talked of going there so I have no idea what it was like but the one run by the entrepreneurial Billy Butlin at Clacton sounded most attractive. My father got a week's paid holiday along with everyone else at Bevan's Cement Works and after a great deal of argument, with my mother maintaining that she would prefer to have a day here and a day there such as Southend-on-Sea and Whipsnade Zoo, Clacton began to be discussed and then quickly discarded once it was realised that all campers were expected to join in the Fun. Apparently we were a family who were not especially good at Fun and so, disappointingly, a week was booked in a boarding house at Ramsgate instead. We paid for bed and breakfast, a cot in the room for my brother, one bath each during the duration of our stay and no eating fish and chips in the room. At least though there seemed to be no compulsory joining in of Fun which reassured my mother.

I no longer remember a great deal about that week except that it was not an unqualified success and the sun did not come out until the day we were leaving. My mother complained a lot about it being impossible to wash and dry nappies and berated me each morning for not eating the breakfast that had been paid for but I was a picky eater and not keen on anything that contained obvious globules of fat which I was always told was the Goodness in the meal and which I most decidedly did not believe. There seemed to be a great deal of Goodness in the slices of black pudding and fried bread on my plate. The grim faced landlady was clearly not overly enthusiastic on her chosen profession and once the guests left the premises after breakfast the front door was firmly locked until five pm when they were reluctantly allowed to return, minus fish and chips and without making undue noise.

The seaside for me meant sticks of rock and sometimes candy floss, brass band music and pebble beaches. I was not at all eager to go on the enforced walks along The Front in gale force winds and longed to be back in York Road playing Hopscotch with Molly. I feared and detested the wheeling gulls, suddenly of an infinitely more massive variety than those that circled the promenade at Gravesend. Their eyes seemed permanently fixed upon me and whatever it was that might be edible about me yet they observed my small brother in a much more benign fashion. Even then and only in his second year of life, his joy at their presence was palpable as he stretched out plump infant arms towards them making earnest sounds in a baby argot that they half seemed to acknowledge. Their hostility was reserved mostly for me so when walking I kept as far away from their sea wall perch as possible and concentrated my thoughts on the ice cream I had been promised. But all ice cream cones appeared to cost sixpence in Ramsgate which was Daylight Robbery and so put on hold in favour of fish and chips. Although eating fish and chips on the beach should have been fun it turned out not to be because of the ongoing proximity of the scavenging gulls. I found myself once again being mercilessly harangued on account of food, this time for not eating my allocated piece of battered hake which was what the avian predators were intent upon taking ownership of. And so I cried bitter tears of frustration and misery and told my long suffering parents that I hated holidays and never again wanted to have one.

By way of compensation and what now stands out as an island of excitement was being taken into a bookshop and being told by my father that I could choose a book to read and to keep. This certainly did not happen very often because I was expected to get all my reading matter from the local library except at Christmas and birthdays when I was sometimes bought second hand books from Gravesend Market. I didn't mind that they were second hand because having my own collection of books was wonderful and made me feel important as I read them again and again. Ramsgate was the only time I remember a new book being purchased, pristine and immaculate from a proper bookshop. My father strongly recommended *Tales From Shakespeare* by some people called Charles and Mary Lamb or *A Child's History of England* by Charles Dickens but to his dismay I firmly rejected both of these ideas and instead spent a long time deliberating the various merits of *The Enid Blyton Book of Fairies* as opposed to *The Enid Blyton Book of Nature*. I finally chose the latter which at six shillings and sixpence also turned out to be Daylight Robbery. All in all it was not a successful holiday which was a pity with it being our very first and my mother said she would be glad to get back to her own bed and holidays were not all they were cracked up to be. What's more she wouldn't be making the same mistake again and she would never have believed the price of things in Ramsgate. She would certainly not complain about Gravesend and Northfleet prices again. If the truth be known, a week by the sea wasn't a patch on Going Hopping and that was a fact.

When we got back to Northfleet, however and people began to ask how our week away at the coast had worked out, I was surprised to find that far from revealing how disastrous it had been she chose to wax lyrical about it and said we were already considering booking for the following year. We might even book early to be sure of getting a good room in the afore-described and previously much maligned guest house. When I protested that I thought she had hated the experience just as much as I had I was told to button my lip because that was no business of anyone else. Only my grandmother and aunts were told the truth and it did not seem to surprise them with Old Nan making comment that Ramsgate and Margate were much overrated and she had never held with them and would sooner go to Southend any day where both the weather and the whelks were glorious. And she agreed that as true as she stood in our kitchen none of these new-fangled seaside guest houses with their fancy prices were a patch on Going Hopping!

Such a disaster was never to happen again and the following year, my Uncle Harold who had become a senior foreman at Dusseks in Crayford and had no fears about using the telephone for the purposes of making holiday bookings, suggested that the entire family should try a week at a place called Swalecliffe at the Hilltop Campsite to be precise. My Grandmother immediately approved and said it was not far from Herne Bay and within easy reach of Whitstable and the delights of everything that Pearsons had to offer and that was a place she remembered well from donkey's years ago. Three chalets and two caravans were duly organised to be shared between us and walks to Tankerton to try the icecream together with visits to Whitstable for oysters and chips were already being excitedly discussed. We four were to occupy one of the caravans which turned out to be called Victoria and was situated directly opposite the much more desirable chalets appropriated early in the piece by Old Nan and various aunts and cousins. The second caravan, called Waterloo, was bigger and generally more impressive than ours and four teenage cousins had immediately taken possession of it. This did not meet with my mother's approval of course but the occupying youths maintained that their heights demanded more room than Victoria offered and then even my father looked affronted.

My mother was definitely Put Out but she said so only to my father who pointed out that if she hadn't agreed to Harold doing the telephoning more claim could have been made to one of the sea-facing chalets. He was perfectly capable of making a telephone call if needs be and that was a fact. Then they had the kind of argument I had become in recent months accustomed to which generally resulted in tears and a long silence followed by my father storming off on his bike. Later I was to understand that he then had a habit of meeting a Fancy Woman at the Ingress Tavern in Stonebridge Road where they had Shrimp Brand beers and was said to have even contrived the conflict in order to keep these appointments. On this occasion, however, he had little chance of doing so as the campsite at Swalecliffe necessitated a rather complicated journey back to Northfleet. Instead he stalked determinedly over to the clifftop and navigated his way down to the cold, windy, pebbly beach and sat hunched against one of the groynes.

Swalecliffe was not by any means perfect and couldn't be compared with Going Hopping but nevertheless our annual holiday for a number of years was to involve the Hilltop Campsite which over time became more acceptable and gradually we were able to rise through the hierarchy somehow and ensure that we occupied one of the cabins rather than Victoria or even Waterloo. Overall each member of the extended Constant family found these sojourns by the sea infinitely preferable to boarding houses in more salubrious parts of the Kent coast. The campsite afforded a great deal more freedom and tolerance for the kind of familial behaviour that came naturally to us, sing-songs and beer drinking after dark for instance, and the occasional robust altercation. To be sure it was conduct that sometimes earned disapproval from other campers and caused comments about Diddicais, but in later years even that would be seen by my brother as merely eccentric and quaintly tribal.

Things were to remain that way for a number of years with a regular group migration of the Constant aunts complete with spouses and offspring from Crayford and Northfleet for the annual invasion of Swalecliffe. 1954 was the fateful year when Aunt Mag, the sister who had always been closest to my mother, suddenly announced she wasn't going to go to that Hilltop Campsite again now that their Margaret was getting married and their Ann growing up so fast too. In fact her Harold had booked for them to go to Weymouth that year, to a very nice boarding house on the Front. A first floor room with All Found and as many baths as you wanted. They might give Hopping a miss too because it wasn't as if they really needed the money now that Harold had got his promotion to Foreman in Chief.

My Aunt was never to be forgiven for this particular piece of perfidy because she had announced it out of the blue and as Bold as Brass with not a thought that Nellie, her widowed sister might like to join them because by then my father had been dead for several years. Oh No never a mention but that was Mag all over. She had never really been one to consider the feelings of others and you only had to think back to that time at Margate before the war and the way she had behaved about the borrowed shoes to get the measure of Mag. Anyway we wouldn't have gone with her even if she'd gone down on bended knee, not for all the tea in China. As far as we were concerned Mag could stick her holiday plans in Weymouth where the sun didn't shine! I mean who would want to go to a dead and alive hole like that anyway? And as for giving Hopping a miss that year, well you could have knocked my mother down with a feather when she said that. She could be a crafty cow at times and it didn't do to trust her and she'd always been one for putting on airs and graces when she'd no reason to. Her Harold liked to throw his weight about too if the truth be known. Well we could go down Hopping on our own couldn't we? We certainly didn't need Mag nor Harold to hold our hands, promotion or no promotion because we were perfectly capable!

And in the end that's what we did, on one of the special Hoppers' Trains from London Bridge that left in the early hours of the morning carrying hundreds of pickers to Paddock Wood, Faversham and Maidstone to the Hop Gardens. We didn't know it at the time but it was the last season of the special trains because the need for hand pickers was fast coming to an end. Old Nan and Little Violet came with us because it turned out that they hadn't been invited to Weymouth either, not that they would have gone even if that cow Mag had begged them to. As we settled into our train journey Old Nan, never slow to lay criticism where it was due, observed that though she said it herself, Mag, her first-born, was at times All Fur Coat and No Knickers. As for that good for nothing Harold of hers, that silly bugger never knew whether he wanted a shit or a haircut. But you couldn't help some people. They wouldn't be told!

Waiting for Womanhood

Bernard first mentioned the various joys of owning peafowl a few days before the horrifying proposed visit of a medical team to Wombwell Hall in mid-1955 and that's why I remember it so well. He said he had recently learned that one of the previous owners of the place had kept a multitude of them and that when you thought about it, it was just the place for them, didn't I agree? There might even be one or two still lurking there. Had I ever come across one? Well I hadn't of course but I was barely listening, so preoccupied was I with what might happen during the fast approaching and greatly dreaded visit of the Health Programme Team to the school. My mother was commenting that she'd been told peacocks made the devil of a noise at four and five in the morning and who would want that? What's more they were prone to shitting all over the place, not to mention ripping up everything in sight. You'd have to really want to keep peacocks to put up with that she thought and if you did you'd only really go in for the cocks with the glorious tail feathers. She couldn't understand why anyone would want the females. I couldn't concentrate on either the good or the bad points of peafowl. It was the horror of medical checks that had me lost in thought.

Such necessities had been a much more simple process in the past. Back in the years that followed World War Two the Nit Nurse regularly visited St Botolph's School, and very likely every other school in the area. It was a visit that mostly we looked forward to because it broke the day to day monotony of Primary School life. But now times had changed and we girls of Wombwell Hall were, we were told, fortunate enough to have the best School Health Programme in the Western World available to us. I was fifteen years old and certainly aware that it was to be an event of some significance because we were warned about it well in advance, reminded about it twice and in addition a note went home with us during the preceding week upon which there was a space for our mothers to write down anything specific about us from a medical viewpoint. That information was to be returned to the office in advance of the visit. I was careful to make sure nothing was written about me by not delivering the note or any reminders in the first place.

It seemed to only be our particular year and not the entire school who were to be subjected to the special event, though we were to have eye and ear checks together with an assessment of our physical development to ensure that we were all progressing in an expected manner. I wasn't the slightest bit concerned about the eye and ear checks but the assessment of our physical development certainly raised some apprehension and I wondered if we were to undergo a test of some kind to prove we were normal. This was largely because I knew I wasn't normal and my lack of normalcy was both mortifying and distressing. It wasn't something that could be discussed easily with friends firstly because I didn't really have any friends that I felt close enough to and secondly because it was a fact so shockingly embarrassing that I was very fearful of being publicly ridiculed on account of it. And in order to avoid the horror of schoolgirl community shame I had already told a number of lies about it, some of them quite extensive. The fact of the matter was that at the great age of fifteen I was destined to go through life as a Non Menstruator, a situation so shameful that even typing it now makes my armpits tingle and my heart beat anxiously a little faster.

My absence of menstruation was definitely at odds with other aspects of my physical development and since my thirteenth birthday men on building sites had been yelling out to me that I had a Lovely Pair. You don't need that at thirteen of course so it didn't actually make me feel any better. Neither did classmates with minimal development themselves who assured me they were envious. Shirley Monroe, measuring us all amid the trees next to the hockey pitch, now a favourite lunchtime occupation, said mine were the biggest in Form 2SC and perhaps I should stop drinking school milk in case they exploded. We were not terribly well informed overall.

This was a time of a complete lack of sex education either at home or at school except a brief session or two called Human Biology in the science programme but it was also a time when, somewhat strangely, girls seemed to share every aspect of growing up with each other and if they had nothing much to share, they made it up. Stories abounded of ten-year-olds in white dresses playing on the swings in Woodlands Park on summer days suddenly and profusely beginning to bleed and having to rush home through throngs of curious Grammar School boys. For some odd reason there were always throngs of Grammar School boys ever watchful in these stories. The distraught girls were invariably comforted by caring older sisters or aunts and put to bed with Aspirin and hot water bottles to ease the physical pain of which there was always a great deal. They also had a stirring tale to share with friends. One by one over several years my schoolmates had each joined the ranks of Becoming Women, even those with no breast development whatsoever. Accordingly whenever the subject was discussed, which was often, I found myself adding to the tales of unbearable pelvic pain and being excused from team games.

You might well wonder why in the light of my well-constructed web of deceit the visit of a school Doctor or Nurse, or both, should concern me in the slightest but the fact was I suspected that they would know simply by looking at me that I was a physical oddity, an aberration like poor Auntie Queenie who my grandmother said was One of Them There Aphrodites and none of us should ever go into a public toilet with her. My affliction was more than likely something hereditary like haemophilia and the apprehension I now felt definitely had something to do with the respect generally afforded the medical profession at that time, a group of special beings with special powers. Perhaps I even had a touch of the same affliction that plagued poor Queenie and it would be immediately obvious to them, maybe such things simply ran in families. I was filled with trepidation because quite clearly I was not a Real Female.

As it happened, when the much dreaded day arrived, despite the combined abilities of the attending doctor who was much younger than any of us expected, and the rather elderly nurse who most of the time seemed to be directing rather than assisting him, it turned out that my lack of growth towards Real Womanhood was not as glaringly obvious as I had suspected. Neither of them seemed to immediately suspect that I was in any way abnormal despite their combined background of medical information.

The Headmistress's study had been turned into a consulting room for the duration of the examinations and she shared her desk with the nurse whilst the young doctor sat uneasily on a folding chair in the centre of the room. On another chair beside him was a pile of pink pamphlets with the title *Growing Towards Womanhood*. As we entered in our underwear Miss Fuller announced us as if we were attending some kind of formal event, by full name then adding our exact age. I was Jean Bernadette Hendy – 15 years and nearly 2 weeks.

My sight and hearing was briefly checked together with my teeth. I was measured and weighed. The nurse simply filled in a vast chart in front of her. The young doctor did not look at me at any stage but most especially when he noted I had 'Well-developed breasts'. Oh the humiliation of that announcement, particularly for someone like me who would have been quite incapable of ordering Chicken Breast at The Chicken Inn had I ever been fortunate enough to be taken there. Breast was a word firmly absent from my vocabulary. Both the nurse and Miss Fuller looked up, alerted by the word, the latter advising me to stand up straight, there was no need to hunch my shoulders. How I despised her with her straight back, in her striped and tidily buttoned blouse with no obvious mammary development whatsoever.

Alert for a possible abnormality to lighten the moment the nurse then wanted to know if my periods were regular and if I experienced any undue pain at which I froze and said nothing at all. Miss Fuller repeated the question slowly and in a voice that indicated she was finding the process just a little tedious but I was still mute, immobile, quite unable to give any reply. The silence that followed seemed endless, all eyes were upon me and I could hear my heart thumping loudly. I stared resolutely out of the window, across the misty park and wondered if the movements in the far distance might be lurking peacocks dancing a slow Pavanne. At last the nurse asked in a slightly more gentle voice if my periods had actually started yet and then I was able to shake my head. She rose from her chair and came over to where I stood, pulling my voluminous forest green winceyette knickers down enough to peer at my private parts and returned to her chair with an obvious waning of interest. She wrote a sentence or two before instructing the doctor that he did not need to give me one of the pink pamphlets as they were only to be given to girls who were already menstruating. I was, she said, a Late Onset Menstruator. Cheeks burning, ears thumping I was then dismissed.

I blame Jill Butler for what happened next, the further and more extensive mortification back in the Science Block as we waited for our usual post Monday morning break class of Human Biology to begin. There was a frisson of anticipation in the room because not only was Miss Norman a forthright and entertaining teacher, we would be discussing The Development of the Human Embryo. Jill Butler, from Burnt Oak Terrace in Gillingham and full of confidence since she became a prefect, wanted to know why I had not been given a pink pamphlet like everyone else. A number of students now sat idly studying them as they waited. I said she should mind her own business because she didn't need to know everything about everybody.

But she was not a girl who gave up easily and sensing a victim she added that at her cousin Brenda's school they had been handed to everyone who had started their periods – the only girls who missed out were those who were in no danger of becoming women any time soon. Surely this must mean that I also fell into that category? Foolishly, as was my habit, I immediately resorted to lying. Why break the habit of a lifetime? Lowering my voice and asking her not to spread the information far and wide I revealed that it was because I only had one ovary. That I thought might shock and silence her but Jill was unstoppable and to my horror she rushed towards the chalk board and wrote in capital letters JEAN HENDY HAS ONLY GOT ONE!

And of course everyone wanted to know what she meant and there was no use hissing at her that I had believed she could be trusted with sensitive information and that only having one while everyone else had two might well mean a number of unpleasant medical procedures were in store for me. The truth of the matter was that Jill quite sensibly did not believe me and was utterly determined to continue the humiliation with clever taunts including comments that she would have thought somebody who wore a size 36 DD bra as she knew I did would have started at eight or nine and not still be still waiting for Womanhood at fifteen! By the time Miss Norman arrived, only two minutes late, most of the remaining class members were dutifully sniggering, and some were laughing uproariously.

If she had left it at that I might even have re-ignited our quasi friendship at some later stage but being Jill, and from her lofty Prefect perch, she was quite unable to let the topic lie and halfway through the Human Biology class when we were drawing embryos and Miss Norman was hovering in our row offering help and advice, she queried in her piercing voice with its stage-like natural projection if it was abnormal for a girl to be born with only one ovary. Miss Norman said she had never really come across it and thought it must indeed be quite unusual.

That lunchtime Jill and I were on plate duty together and I took the opportunity to tearfully tell her that I would never, ever trust her with confidential information again, that she was totally unreliable. She said she'd rather be unreliable than a complete weirdo like me with tits like mine. She said it was called Abnormal Breast Development. And so then I hated her even more and visualised her being pecked to death by peafowl as she scraped plates with unusual energy.

I left early that day without asking for permission and nobody noticed. The driveway down into Hall Road was completely empty and strangely silent. There were no peafowl to be seen.

The Peep Toe Shoes

That day when I told Miss Fuller that I was unaware that peep toe shoes were not acceptable footwear for Wombwell Hall I was, for once, telling the truth. We were both looking at the shoes in question at the time and it was only just beginning to dawn on me that I was in fact in breach of the uniform rules and that the violation had been going on for almost that entire term. There were three weeks to go before the Christmas break and we were already deep into the daily practice of appropriate Carols of which my favourite was definitely *Oh Little Town of Bethlehem*. My brother had been insisting for several weeks that a robin was nesting in an old kettle long abandoned at the end of Old Maudie's back yard further down York Road despite the local cats. As Christmastime approached he was anxious for robins and snow and the Salvation Army Band. My mother was hopeful as usual that the festive season would pass without unpleasantness and already regretting that we were going to stay with her sister Rose in Yorkshire married to Mervyn who was known to be careful with money. I was looking forward to time out of school when reading could be done and future plans made. Breaching school rules was not one of them.

Miss Fuller looked slightly irritated when, because my mind was straying, she had to ask me twice if I had alternative footwear available. I hastily told her that yes I did even though this was a lie unless you counted too tight summer sandals passed down by my cousin Connie and Wellington boots. I knew neither were an option for daily wear to Wombwell Hall. I hoped she would not remember that it was the second time I had stood before her for breaking shoe rules and in fact she didn't seem to. She looked up from the chart on the desk in front of her and stared directly into my eyes, stopping herself from demanding that I look at her when she was speaking in the nick of time because by a mere millisecond I already was. Instead she told me that she need not remind me that I was a Fully Funded for Uniform Pupil. I nodded agreement and she added that there was really no excuse for me to be wearing the forbidden peep toe shoes and I hastily agreed and wondered what was wrong with them considering that they fitted the required colour option of brown or black. They were black and well-polished. There was still a lot of wear left in them even though I had a tendency to Roll Over the left foot which rendered the level of the sole uneven.

I was always accused of being Hard on footwear and my mother only wished Old Hammond the cobbler could fit metal clinks like in the old days but he'd told her they were only used for work boots in the thoroughly modern 1950s. I didn't mention any of this to Miss Fuller of course, knowing perfectly well that she would not be interested being a woman unlikely to ever have encountered a clink on a work boot. The Headmistress was always fair and it was not as if I was constantly hauled before her for misdemeanours but she was also Posh in the way that those who went into teaching back in those days and rose significantly were. She was also stylish and wore tweed suits with gored skirts and cream silk blouses. Her hair was short enough for my mother to describe her as Mannish and her own shoes were as highly polished as mine but sensibly laced and of course without any vestige of a peep toe about them. Her voice always seemed to be hiding behind her teeth and when she spoke she sounded a bit like the military men in the films my mother liked so much about officers escaping from prisoner of war camps in World War Two. In fact there was no doubt that she was not the most feminine of women but this applied to more than one of those entering the teaching profession in my opinion and I had already decided it was a consequence of some aspects of higher education, probably Mathematics. She was telling me that as I had alternative footwear she did not want to see the peep toe shoes again and to remember that I was Fully Funded so I nodded enthusiastically and assured her it would not happen again. I did, however, hope my mother would not get too angry about it all and wondered what I would wear the following day.

I need not have worried at all because the next day was a Friday and instead of going to school I was taken on the 480 to Dartford to Dolcis Shoes where my cousin Margaret was now working. Bernard wanted a day off school too and whined about being allowed to come with us but he was told the answer was definitely No. In any case we would be back in the shake of a gnat's whisker and if by chance we weren't he was to wait quietly by the Anderson and behave himself and to button his lip if any nosy parker neighbour asked why. So we went without him and bought proper school shoes with sturdy soles and long laces and I was allowed to choose either black or brown so I chose black. Then we had cups of tea and biscuits in the café over the road because Margaret was entitled to a forty five minute lunch break. We paid for the café treat because Margaret had managed to organise for us to get the shoes at sale price even though the sale did not start for another week.

In the cafe Margaret talked about the Wednesday evening typing class she was doing in order to better herself and my mother talked about schools having a Bloody Cheek telling students what kind of shoes they should be wearing and how women like that Miss Fuller didn't know their arses from their elbows and those peep toe shoes still had plenty of wear left in them. I talked about not really understanding what Fully Funded for Uniform really meant even though of course I did, and was pleased to note my mother's discomfiture. I even elaborated and said Miss Fuller had explained that Fatherless pupils were considered Orphans and so a regular sum was awarded to us so that all our uniform needs could be fully met. This meant, I said that expensive items like regulation cardigans could be purchased with ease from the Uniform Shop in Gravesend. My mother said there was plenty of wear left in the school cardigan she had knitted for me in exactly the right shade of Forest Green and she wasn't made of money.

My brother said that while he was waiting for us after school he'd persuaded Old Maudie to let him examine the kettle at the bottom of her yard. There was no sign of the robin though and he thought her cat might have got to it.

A Need For Plumed Horses

Burial places are of more importance to some people than to others. There was a time when you could definitely rely on having a designated location where the dead could be visited if you leaned towards significance. Some families did not take advantage of this sensible custom and ours was one of them; where the dead rested in eternal peace simply did not seem to concern us terribly much. Not that they were forgotten altogether, of course. Very far from it. Whenever we passed Dartford Cemetery on the 480 bus on our way to Northfleet my grandmother would comment that her Poor Arthur lay within and after a second or two, as if pausing to remember salient facts might add that her first Arthur was there with him too. Usually these remarks fell into the air, and were greeted with silence but once I ventured to ask how old her Arthurs were when they died. Then she straightened her shoulders a bit and said it was beyond her to remember and they were just wee mites. As she had given birth to a multitude of children it might not have been altogether odd that her memory for those who perished as infants was not as sharp as it might have been. Decades later when he was already in his sixties my brother said that in his opinion she harboured a great deal of guilt for the one, or maybe two, that were the victims of her drunkenness and thus found dead in the marital bed. He reminded me with an air of satisfaction that it was that very fact that led to our grandfather, Edgar Constant, giving up alcohol altogether. Sadly Old Nan never exhibited the same moral fortitude as her husband and continued to drink throughout her life.

I wondered if it was in fact her own culpability that prevented her from pausing by the infant gravesides from time to time but Bernard disagreed and said it was because we simply were not a family that set much store by graves. When I became an adult I began to understand that burial places are far more than places to conveniently house the dead. Within them we are exposed to a precise and accurate reflection of social, economic and ethnic history and so much of this information can be missed when they are bypassed because they allow us to step effortlessly into the past. They also contain a treasury of fascinating personal stories where the pain of past families losing children to illness and lovers to war is brought abruptly into focus. Life's injustices are exposed and the inequalities between rich and poor are forever evident. And even for those totally uninterested in these aspects of social history they at least offer quiet places in which to walk or sit and read a book or eat a lunchtime sandwich. And they are certainly permanent wildlife centres where an extraordinary range of fauna can be seen.

For me as I grew to adulthood they became places where I established a closer relationship with those I would have so much liked to have known in life – in Brompton Cemetery Emmeline Pankhurst and Richard Tauber, in Highgate Karl Marx, Radclyffe Hall and George Eliot, in Chiswick William Hogarth and James Whistler and in Bunhill Fields John Bunyan, William Blake and Daniel Defoe. Without the restraining influence of my uninterested family I so rapidly became a graveyard devotee.

The post-war years was a time when the majority of people in the community had a more intimate relationship with relatives no longer living than they might these days so our family was very different in that we rarely went in for regularly visiting memorials to relatives. I came to accept our catalogue of dissimilarities and decided it was because we were more common and vulgar than the decent poor around us. I don't recall ever being taken to the last resting place of the Constant infants neither to those of their four or five sisters who succumbed to Tuberculosis as young adults. It seemed that although no expense was spared when it came to funerals and it was rumoured that Old Nan insisted on splashing out on plumed horses on one occasion, extending the relationship with top-up visits to the departed was not deemed necessary. In fact our grandmother could be quite matter-of-fact about family deaths and busied herself with what she saw as essential rituals such as burning all the combustible possessions of the deceased that had not been claimed by the living. Items of value such as pieces of jewellery were passed on but generally bed linen, clothing, etc was burned. My mother felt that all this burning had something to do with the passing on of infection when it was a young person who had died but had little to offer on the topic when it was pointed out that fires took place regardless of age. I knew her mind was on the greatly feared spectre of TB. I wondered a little uneasily if books would also have also been tossed onto the pyres because she definitely believed that library books might hold the kernel of the disease within their pages but I never found out as few of my relatives were inclined towards reading.

Nevertheless I could not help but notice that other families did not seem to go in for ritual fires, more items were passed on and once the grieving period was over a distinctive relationship developed between the dead and their still-living relatives, an association that nowadays barely seems to exist in quite the same way. York Road children regularly accompanied parents or grandparents to Northfleet cemetery and viewed the pursuit as an activity they largely looked forward to or at the very least did not mind too much. Molly from No 31 once said it was a pity that she and I did not seem to have any dead relatives and that she for one envied Rita Jenkins. Rita was invariably in a smart Sunday outfit complete with Dutch bonnet sporting appliqued felt flowers when she and her grandmother made the weekly trip to visit her grandfather. In Molly's opinion it was because she was an only child and everyone knew single child parents went in for a lot of spoiling.

When I ventured to ask if we could go visiting at the cemetery my mother shuddered and said she didn't hold with it, that the dead should be left in peace and managed to make it sound as if she thought they were better left to their own devices and that intruding was just downright rude. However, I knew that she was in fact particularly alarmed by the idea of death, especially when contemplating her own and according to her sisters, who had always taken delight in taunting her, had always felt the same.

It was Mrs Bassant who finally said that if we liked to do so Molly and I could accompany her and her granddaughter Evelyn to visit her older sister, Poor Ada who had become a victim to the Great Flu that followed the Great War. Although neither of us felt particularly friendly towards Evelyn, who was an unfortunately overweight girl and easily bullied, we enthusiastically agreed. Evelyn was not quite as keen on the idea as her grandmother as it had not been long since the incident of the cricket bat that she had found on the Old Green and that I had deftly removed from her possession by falsely claiming that the finder was actually me. However as the Sunday of the visit approached and as I had been friendly towards her for several days in a row her fears abated and she seemed to almost be looking forward to the event. She importantly explained to both Molly and me that she would be in charge of getting the water for the flowers but that we could help and she would show us how it was done and where the best tap was. She warned us that we might have to queue. She also told us that Granny always took shortbread and sugared almonds along for a mid-afternoon snack and we would be able to share in the treat. We were most definitely looking forward to it.

   On Sunday morning Evelyn and I were detailed to pick a large bunch of gladioli from the startling array planted by Mr Bassant in the back yard adjacent to the old Anderson shelter. These were to be placed on Poor Ada's grave directly after Sunday dinner which Evelyn said was always a cold one on cemetery days to save time and energy. We walked to the cemetery, down the steep hill over the railway bridge and past Gemmel's Farm and the little farm cottages on the right, then past the allotments on the left where Mr Bassant was a tenant and grew vegetables very successfully as he had done throughout the war years. Molly's mother always said that we would never have got by without starving if it hadn't been for Mr Bassant's horticultural expertise and generosity. She didn't say it quite like that but that is what she meant because his prize marrows were astonishing and lasted for days.

Evelyn was wearing a smart polka-dot dress with a matching sunhat that had been made for her recent birthday. Molly and I were especially nice to her and in fact felt quite shabby as we walked beside her and Molly even told her that she wasn't nearly as fat as some people said she was; she was just a little on the stout side. Evelyn said thank you and in any case she wasn't really fat because it was a glandular problem.

When we got to the cemetery it was almost but not quite a veritable hive of activity. Along each row of graves women of mostly grandmotherly age knelt, some on cushions like the ones you find in church, and dug with miniature tools or pulled up weeds. Some were accompanied by men who seemed to be quite uncharacteristically doing their wife's bidding and many had children of various ages with them who seemed to be doing the same. It was the children who staggered back and forth from the taps set around the building in the central area that looked just a little like a fairy tale cottage but wasn't because Evelyn said it was a Records Office. The children, each with a watering can, queued patiently at the taps for their quota of water, the boys always overfilling their cans. There was a great deal of noise but very little quarrelling except from pre-schoolers arguing that they were not too young to help. Evelyn meticulously filled the first can very nearly to the brim and Molly had to help her carry it back to pour on Poor Ada. Then she generously said it was my turn so I smiled and thanked her politely and even for a fleeting moment thought of returning the cricket bat to her.

As they worked, these industrious visitors conversed effortlessly with each other, directing a comment or two to the dead and a great many to the child helpers. Mrs. Giles whose house was between ours and Molly's said she only wished she had a willing kiddy to help her and she certainly would have had by now if any of her girls had married which none of them had. Molly whispered to me that it was unclear which girl now lay peacefully at her feet but she had a feeling it had been the dreaded TB that had made off with her. Old Mrs Mannering from Tooley Street arrived later than us, hurrying and wheezing as she did so, complaining that her Sidney always wanted a roast of a Sunday, cemetery or no cemetery. Mrs Bassant said she should simply provide something cold on visiting days and let him get on with it but Mrs Mannering said that would cause him to get the Hump and he got the Hump easily enough as it was.

When the gladioli had been arranged in their glass pot and all the weeds on Poor Ada's grave had been deftly removed, we three girls were given shortbread and sugared almonds to share just as Evelyn had promised. We sat on the steps of the fairy tale cottage to eat them and then helped the biggest boys to stack the watering cans tidily against what Evelyn told us was the north wall. It had been a most satisfactory outing and when we got home I immediately broached the subject of a Sunday in the cemetery once again with my mother but she was unresponsive and said a lot of time could be wasted in such places and she had better things to do which wasn't what I wanted to hear at all.

Little more than a year later my father's sudden death was to bring us face to face with the very place she had so determinedly tried to avoid. For several months we at last became part of that group of weekend visitors I had so desired to join and my brother and I were able to carry cans of water back and forth from the taps and arrange flowers in a jar just as I had hoped and I was even able to talk importantly about the visits at school. The gloss seemed to wear off remarkably rapidly however and perhaps that was because community attitudes were changing fast and a dedication to the dead was losing its attraction in our corner of North Kent. The tide was definitely turning for routine grave visiting and over the following years the rows of memorial plots that had once been regularly tended with such dedication, became unkempt and uncared for. The local population now emulated those sentiments that had long been present in the Constant Family and no longer felt it necessary to commune so frequently with those who had passed. It was as if a tsunami of Constant rejection for reverence had now spilled out into the lives of ordinary and more decent people, those who had never had to live in fear of being called Diddicais. Along with the trend a whole raft of human experience was being discarded and those family members who no longer lived among us lost a great deal of the importance they had once had in our lives. They were spoken of less frequently and only emerged in old photographs in dusty albums when someone might point out that Little Vera had her Great Aunt Edna's eyes.

Long decades later my brother told me that when he was a child he had often wondered why our father's grave seemed to mean so little to us and had decided that the lack of attention to it was ruled by an ingrown acceptance of tribal neglect exacerbated by poverty. That might of course have been true. Bernard had spent a great deal of time in Northfleet Cemetery when he was growing up simply because he said it was an excellent place to see birds and owls in particular. He had glimpsed not only Tawny Owls but once a Barn Owl, not to mention the less frequently seen Little Owl, just six inches high, yellow eyed with an immediately recognisable bobbing head. In later years groups of Feral Parakeets made these now neglected environs their home and caused a flurry of excitement among local ornithologists.

By then, however, we had both well and truly emerged from our poverty stricken childhood and I had married a New Zealand doctor to my mother's great satisfaction and my brother was on the brink of becoming extremely rich. Our father's grave had by the year 2000 long welcomed our mother and lay as abandoned and uncared for as ever it threatened to be back in 1953. When Bernard died himself in April 2016 quite strangely his wife although she had no Constant blood whatsoever, decided not to go in for either a funeral or a grave. This bizarre decision ricocheted through family and friends who all knew he would have expected and very much liked to have had the former. Briefly I could even see why it was that when she could afford them, plumed horses had been important to Old Nan. A funeral procession like those that are still occasionally seen in the East End of London when an infamous felon or a notable Romany takes his leave from the community would have had enormous appeal to Bernard as a valediction of his significance to those he loved and who loved him, but it was not to be. He would not have set nearly as much store by a grave though. There was a long line of Constants in him after all.

A Conspiracy of Ravens

Our local Lunatic Asylum was called Stone House and was situated at Stone quite close to Dartford. It was built in the eighteen sixties specifically for the insane of the area. A menacing looking place, designed in what was described as a Tudor Revival style by James Bunstone Bunning, it was rumoured that a pair of Ravens had lived there from the very day it had opened. Old Mrs Giles said a pair was called an Unkindness of Ravens and claimed to have caught a glimpse of them when passing on the top deck of the bus. I didn't altogether believe her because she had once declared she had seen Satan disguised as a Rag & Bone man one Sunday afternoon in Tooley Street. In any case at that stage I had no understanding of collective nouns and didn't know what was meant by the mysterious Unkindness she spoke of. Apart from all that though, as the only Ravens I was familiar with lived in the Tower of London, I was nevertheless quite fascinated. Once I stumbled upon the pages of Edgar Allan Poe I was even more entranced.

Whenever we passed Stone House either on the bus or on foot my mother would shudder and, showing a modicum of compassion which was unusual for her, comment that it must be dreadful to end up there and she pitied those poor souls locked up inside. When I mentioned the Ravens she said they were probably crows and went back to shuddering. Aunt Mag said it was well known that Ravens were dodgy buggers and could certainly give rabbits a run for their money and during the Great War they had even been known to hunt down cats to kill and eat them. I wondered if there was a Stone House cat and if so, did it realise that it might be in danger of becoming bird prey. I was certainly more concerned about the possible fate of the cat than the well-being of the inmates. Back then, there wasn't a great deal of patience or understanding from anyone for those afflicted with mental illness let alone people as young as me.

In the totally modern 2020s we have developed a much more relaxed attitude that could even be said to border on blasé. We are decidedly Cool about psychiatric illness, and keen to accept all manner of unusual behaviour that years ago would have seen us definitely concerned. I'm old enough to remember the horrified whispers that followed Poor Pauline Prentice around Northfleet High Street simply because she had a tendency to remove items of clothing in public, particularly if she had to wait too long in the queue at Ripley's the greengrocer. Even Aunt Queenie called it Shameful and as most of the other aunts agreed, Queenie had little to boast about herself as far as shame was concerned.

In Coronation Year tolerance was thin on the ground for those who couldn't pull themselves together after having a baby or who claimed to feel so despondent about life that they took to their beds on a semi-permanent basis. Just imagine if we all did that! On the other hand there were times when something called a Nervous Breakdown, which people do not suffer from these days, was called for such as when the young husband of one of my older cousins simply went to pieces when she left him. His despair and the reasons for it were certainly recognised but there was no rush to his side to offer assistance or to counsel him. In fact there was a tacit acceptance that it was better by far to stay well away until he came to his senses. His behaviour was seen as unacceptable and it was better by far to ignore it because even more scandalous was the fact that the marriage had crumbled in the first place. After all that money had been spent on it and her poor father working those extra shifts down at Vickers even with that bad back of his. It didn't bear thinking about.

Because I was what my mother called Fanciful it did not take long for me to firmly associate all variants of mental disturbance with Ravens and to this day I still do, pairs of them hovering on the fringes of every radio discussion or every informative magazine article. Of course back in the mid-1950s there were no radio or television talk programmes advising the afflicted on how best to cope, no self-help groups where pressing problems might be discussed, simply the glaringly obvious social ignominy that announced to the world that the sufferer did not have sufficient backbone to deal with adversity. As a group of average working class citizens we definitely lacked empathy and I clearly recall one neighbour making the comment to another that she didn't have much time for recently bereaved Lil Shrimpton who couldn't even behave herself at her own sister's funeral, and wept like a baby. What a way to behave! And following Uncle Paddy's unfortunate fatal accident celebrating the end of the war, within a month Aunt Martha was reprimanded by her sisters for still being tearful for surely to goodness weeping day and night wasn't going to change things was it?

Perhaps the stiffness of those upper lips in times past had something to do with the fear of ending up in dark and hostile places of care like Stone House even though some of those structures distinguished themselves by harbouring exotic birds of myth and legend. We children called them Loony Bins and jeered at others who had relatives incarcerated within although I stopped doing so when I discovered that my paternal grandmother had been a long term patient at Barming Heath near Maidstone. My father didn't call it Barming Heath but instead referred to it as Oakwood Hospital but he did so in a low voice. My mother only discussed it with folded arms and tightly pursed lips and said it was the need to go into such a place that had led to my poor father being brought up in a children's home from the age of four, dear innocent little soul. He on the other hand always maintained that the children's home hadn't given him an entirely bad childhood. But there was no convincing my mother who thought that flighty good-for-nothing older sister of his, Connie, should have taken care of him even if she did turn out to be merely a half-sister in the end. Blood's thicker than water after all – or it should be. The fact that Connie was only fifteen years old herself was immaterial. Such a thing would never have happened among the Constants where completely abandoning a child of the family was unheard of.

For my grandmother it was not Stone House that meandered across restless dreams complete with fluttering Corvids, but Colney Hatch, once the biggest institution in Europe, housing almost three thousand patients. As a three-year-old I was already aware that at times my behaviour was in danger of driving her there because she told me so and although I had no idea where this place of horrors might be I was mindful that I should tread more carefully to avoid her or anyone else in the family ending up there. Later I learned it was just North of London, but near a crossroads which was always a bad sign for some reason, and had at one time housed the wife of Aleister Crowley and also someone suspected of being Jack the Ripper. These facts were moderately interesting but once I became a student at Wombwell Hall and had fallen in love with Miss K Smith, certainly not as noteworthy as her announcing that our very own Stone House had been home for years to the famous war poet, Ivor Gurney. I didn't like to ask her what category of unacceptable behaviours had led to his incarceration. Had he wept too copiously at a sibling's funeral perhaps? Did he have a habit of removing items of clothing if forced to wait too long in queues? Eventually I read somewhere that he had suffered from something called Manic Depression but I had little idea what that entailed and certainly didn't believe whoever it was who told me that it could be easily cured with electric currents through the brain.

As time passed and attitudes towards mental health issues underwent a change, being incarcerated in places like Stone House became less of a reality and although our mother still shivered theatrically when the place was mentioned, my aunts showed no interest whatsoever and my brother's only interest revolved around whether or not the Ravens I had told him about were still there. Had Britain's most legendary bird actually returned to the South of England? There was a time, he told me, just a couple of hundred years previously, when they had been widespread across the British Isles but persecution by the gamekeepers of the Victorian era had all but destroyed their population. Bernard by this time was ten, and had become ever more preoccupied with ornithology. He informed me that these members of the crow family were uniquely intelligent, fantastic mimics and he would so much like to own one. When I mentioned that keeping one might be quite unkind he said that they loved, more than anything else, interacting with people so they would welcome being owned. I have no idea whether that assertion had any truth in it.

It was to be many years before we spoke again of Ravens, then via a long distance telephone conversation in the days of fax machines and direct dialling around the globe but before mobile phones, texts and emails. Our mother had begun to exhibit signs of dementia and was to be Assessed in the very place that had previously held so many fears for her, the greatly dreaded Stone House. We discussed those fears and wondered if she still had any memory and knowledge of them. Had her qualms ever in fact been entirely rational? Would the idea of an assessment carried out in that terrible place fill her with even greater trepidation and anxiety? Would it perhaps remain just a half-worry from a time that no longer had any reality or substance in the context of life in the frenzied 1980s? Had the Asylum, the Loony Bin become merely an insubstantial fragment of times past like the Workhouse or the Village Stocks or being Transported to Australia?

We spoke for a long time and although I doodled a procession of Ravens across the notepad beside the telephone, we reached no conclusion. Eventually Bernard said he hoped the birds were still there, not just one or two but perhaps three or even four. A Conspiracy of Ravens, he added after a short silence, certainly not an Unkindness.

The Truth Behind Plagues of Parakeets

A great deal of quite colourful language has been lost over the years and I suppose we have to accept this fact because we all know that over time language changes – if it did not reliably do so we would all still be speaking Chaucer's English. Unlike my grandmother, few women of her ilk these days are regularly about to be Struck Pink or Knocked Down by a Feather. Her only son, my ever jovial Uncle Edgar, always became Tickety Boo when he'd had a couple of pints at the Jolly Farmers and he mystifyingly went off to See a Man About a Dog several times each week despite the fact that the canine never eventuated. His daughter Daphne confided that he had never been known to harbour any true fondness for dogs and the closest she got to any family pet was the Ring Necked Parakeet he brought home from the pub one Friday evening. She even wondered if it had been exchanged for the much-discussed dog and for a while made a decision not to like it as a protest. Aunt Mag sensibly commented that at least it seemed quite friendly which was a bonus because they could be vicious sods. Parakeets were still something of a novelty and buyers were warned they could be dangerous. There might have been something in that as we now know that in some areas they are said to terrorise whole neighbourhoods descending in flocks to alarm small children in local parks.

My mother was eventually to blame the Great Storm of 1987 for the aerial bombardment of Wallis Park, and said Northfleet had become a Dead and Alive Place and that was a fact. She did not subscribe to the idea that a number of pop stars might be to blame for the rogue parakeet problem. However, this was all to come and back in 1949 she was still talking about old Mr Bassant knowing his onions when it came to mending a door frame or changing a fuse. Somehow or other I realized that the onions under discussion were not those very same ones he grew on his allotment.

This vast array of now almost forgotten expressions was part of an accepted web of communication that all children growing up in the Thameside towns of North Kent were totally familiar and comfortable with. We all knew that Bob was our Uncle and Fanny was our Aunt. We accepted that Brass Monkeys had a lot to do with low temperatures. Cock Ups were not in any way lewd and we didn't whine for attention when we knew the adults around us were Knackered. A Nod was always as good as a Wink and some people could be As Keen as Mustard. Little Birds often informed my mother and aunts on vital information and there was a lot of excitement locally if someone decided to Have a Do. In fact with neighbourly help general preparations could be carried out in Two Shakes of a Gnat's Whisker.

Along with this disappearing argot a lively collection of ethnic slurs that would today horrify were apt to effortlessly trip off the tongue and we were largely unaware of the racist connotations. Those racial groups being maligned also seemed mostly oblivious to insult and cheerfully accepted being known as Jocks and Micks and

Krauts. It was some time before I fully understood the latter term because it seemed to spring out of nowhere following the war years, completely sweeping away Hun, its fully comprehended predecessor.

Old Nan, always at the forefront where offensive conduct was concerned, was unembarrassed to refer to the local jeweller as a Kike and to the new Jamaican immigrants as Coons which looking back was a line her daughters seemed reluctant to cross. To my grandmother this lexicon was merely useful descriptive language and she might well have expressed considerable surprise to be reprimanded for it. Throughout my childhood, when faced with an uncooperative grandchild she would dole out a hefty clip around the ear and tell us we were being Proper Tartars or Right Bleeding Brahmans! She would have been quite unaware that the former are an ethnic group still living in the Volga-Ural region and that the vast majority of them are Muslim. Nor would she have cared. As for the latter, where she acquired the term Brahman remains a mystery but she certainly would have been unaware of the fact that they are considered the highest Hindu caste and responsible for teaching and maintaining sacred knowledge. To her a Brahman was simply an uppity child in need of stern rebuke coupled with a painful clout. My brother, once he had become fully involved in the dissection of family history, decided that her frequent use of the term had something to do with the fact that her own mother had been born in India and thus would have brushed against the caste system at one time or another. How much validity this supposition had is debatable but it would be interesting to know where some of the more extravagant terms and phrases used by Old Nan Constant actually came from.

In these more progressive times when the morbidly obese object to being described as Overweight and those lacking vision can no longer safely be called Blind, one can only view with amazement what the average man/woman/person in the street once got away with. In primary school playgrounds Asian children had long been immune to being described as Chinks, Nips or Japs and would have been unlikely to be affronted. Even the youngest among us understood such terms and for most of us they simply indicated an acceptance that a particular group might differ from the majority but were still safely part of the larger community.

There was surprisingly little confusion although I can recall asking my father what the difference was between a Wop and a Wog at the age of about seven and him explaining that a Wop was simply another word for an Italian and a Wog was a more general term for someone with a dark skin. There was no sharp intake of breath coupled with a look over the shoulder, no speaking in a hushed whisper. He would have been perplexed if told that within his children's lifetime the word Eskimo would have developed unpleasant connotations and that the Englishmen who had served alongside him in the Eighth Army most of whom had grown quite fond of being called Limeys were beginning to feel slighted when described as Poms. He would have been bewildered to be told that Cretins and Cripples no longer existed along with Imbeciles and that referring to those from Pakistan as Pakkis was a definite No-No!

There is nothing very surprising about any of this but losing language that was once fully integrated within a functioning society can surprise and startle and leave the speaker groping for alternatives. Who could have anticipated that the expression No Can Do would become clearly contemptuous of the manner in which the immigrant Chinese once used English? And could men like my father have possibly foreseen that Long Time No See holds the Native Americans' traditional greeting up to scorn and ridicule? Could my mother have taken seriously the fact that by using one of her most favoured invectives – Bugger – she was actually referring to Bulgarian sodomites? And how would she have reacted if called upon to explain herself for describing Little Old Maudie from a few doors along as Feeble Minded? After all everyone knew Little Old Maudie was Feeble Minded and that's precisely why her neighbours looked out for her and made sure she wasn't exploited by Them Buggers involved in doorstep selling.

A great deal has been lost along with swathes of now unacceptable terminology but the campaigners for its demise are clearly more absorbed with the possible suffering of those who might find parts of it offensive for an increasing number of reasons. Customs and traditions linked to a disappearing way of life are of minor importance and in the overall scheme of things who can argue about that?

What in the first place might have instigated this now rampant aversion to once acceptable language is already lost to legend and when it is discussed a range of outlandish theories are offered. Perhaps there is some similarity in the origin of Britain's Plagues of Parakeets –

was it Jimi Hendrix releasing a breeding pair called Adam & Eve? Or George Michael? Or was the real culprit Humphrey Bogart? Did the birds simply escape from the set of *The African Queen*? New research, however, reveals that Parakeet sightings actually date back to the 1880s and one study reports that it was actually 1855!

I daresay we will never know the truth.

Birds of Prey

There were two doctors in Northfleet, Dr Crawford and Dr Outred, and you swore by whichever one of them you favoured and that very much depended on how much you considered they had done for your family and whether they had ever gone above and beyond the Call of Duty. They were invariably known simply by their surnames. We swore by Outred rather than Crawford because he was renowned for being able to do surgery if needs be and more importantly had saved my life when I was four. He didn't actually perform surgery upon me but he drove at breakneck speed to Gravesend Hospital to access what he called a Wonder Drug when I had pneumonia. I was busy watching relays of dancing Dutch dolls climb the walls of my bedroom and by the time he returned was not aware enough to know how I felt about the size of the needle he used. According to my mother it was enormous! Needless to say with the aid of the Wonder Drug I quickly recovered and rather generously bore him no grudges about the needle. As for surgery, he had at one stage lanced a nasty throat abscess for my mother whilst bombs rained down on his consulting room in London Road, Northfleet, at least that is how she described the occasion and at one time she described it a great deal.

Aunt Mag said that when all was said and done you could quite understand why Nell swore by him. However, she stopped all the swearing once she came to understand that he had been complicit in my father's death by not realizing that he was suffering from Acute Hepatitis rather than some kind of fairly harmless seasonal influenza. It was my Grandmother and the combined efforts of the Aunts that finally convinced her that the once much revered Outred was undoubtedly responsible for the unexpected and most inconvenient sudden death. Even way back then there were those who were keen on a place to lay blame when faced with some of life's slings and arrows. We had not got to the stage, however, where we demanded apologies; we simply seethed with indignation at the injustice of it all. My poor mother seethed a great deal because at the time of the death that by rights should never have happened she was not altogether on speaking terms with my father. This was because she could not forgive him for being a serial philanderer. Later she maintained that it was The War that was responsible for the philandering and the Eighth Army in particular because that was where his fascination for women in uniform began and had it not been for that he would never have looked twice at any of the clippies on the 480 bus route.

As a child I spent a reasonable amount of time in Outred's waiting room, most especially once the National Health System was up and running and we no longer had to pay for each visit. Prior to the NHS every consultation had to be paid for and I remember that for an adult this was a costly two shillings and sixpence because it was indignantly discussed frequently. I'm no longer sure what was charged for children. There was general dissatisfaction when a half crown had to be handed over despite no firm diagnosis being made and my mother was most satisfied when she was prescribed a Tonic, preferably a red one in an interesting glass bottle. The red Tonics did her a lot of good, of that she was certain.

Outred did not run an appointments system which was undoubtedly sensible as telephones were largely absent in working class households, but he did run two surgeries per day, morning and afternoon. You simply turned up and sat on one of the hard wooden chairs and tried to be quiet if you were a child which was difficult if the wait was a particularly long one. If you were an adult you could speak to those around you if you so wished. There were no toys and books to amuse younger patients as would be usual these days. This would have been a forward thinking initiative had Outred been forward thinking enough to think of it but it was clear he regarded most of his child patients as future delinquents and was disinclined to provide benevolent diversions. Following the incident of the redistribution of pills I was involved in when I was too young to fully comprehend the consequences of what I was doing, he did not trust me one iota and I came to accept that. I can't say I blame him and fortunately for me the said incident took place after he so valiantly saved my life and had it not done so I do have to wonder about the outcome of that bout of pneumonia. I won't go into all the unhappy details as the particular tale of woe has been fully documented elsewhere but it would never have happened had I not been left alone in the waiting room whilst my mother discussed something personal with him. As I had at the time an over-developed sense of what was fair I simply wanted to make sure everyone got at least some of the brightly coloured pills that had been left for collection by the sick. It seemed grossly unjust to me that some people only got white ones. None of this reasoning went down well with our medical man.

In my defence, and although I don't want to labour the point, things might not have progressed to the redistribution of medicines had our doctor gone in for providing one or two amusements for child patients. The only diversion he did have was a series of framed prints on the walls of the waiting room. British Birds of Prey! The Glorious Golden Eagle, Falcon in Flight, Common Buzzard Cruising, Descending Sparrowhawk and Hovering Kestrel. By the time I was seven years old I could confidently read the captions beneath each picture and my favourite was Falcon in Flight because the terrain below looked almost like local farmer, that Bastard Beasley's pea fields. According to my grandmother Farmer Beasley failed to pay the going rate when he hired pickers in early June and therefore could be viewed with disdain and spoken of with derision using any expletive you chose.

The London Road waiting room could only be described as functional, with a disparate collection of chairs jammed close together against three of the walls. There was a no-longer-wanted dining table in the middle of the room, highly polished but with only a vase of flowers in the centre and three ashtrays around the edges. Mrs Outred was fond of flowers and grew a great many in her garden even in wartime when we all knew she should have switched to onions and carrots and she generally remembered to ring the changes with what was in the vase. Against the fourth wall was a tall, narrow side table and by late afternoon an array of jars and bottles sat on it carefully labelled for patients to collect. It was this table that had proved too enticing for me to ignore as a pre-school warrior for justice. So single minded had I been that I had to drag over an empty chair to climb on – a demanding task but the execution of it exhilarating.

There was no receptionist and as patients arrived they simply seated themselves where they felt comfortable and remembered who was in the queue before them. Mistakes were seldom made. As each consultation ended and the object of it hurried out into London Road with head down, a little brass bell on the wall above the tall, narrow side table tinkled and whoever was next in line headed along the short, dark corridor to the consulting room. If you were unsure of the direction or lost your way you could look on the wall where an arrow and a sign in what had once been gold lettering read – Consulting Room This Way.

The reason for the frequent seeking of medical attention for me once the NHS was well and truly up and running and there was no chance of money changing hands was because I had always been Delicate. I was also Highly Strung. I recall with clarity family and neighbours being advised that it was the doctor himself who had pronounced this which was in point of fact quite incorrect. It was apparently impossible to feed me which was at least partly true and had more to do with the end of strict wartime rationing than fragility of constitution. I had become happily accustomed to a plain fat-free wartime diet which by 1948 had morphed into a great many fried items and stews top heavy with mutton fat which was food that met with my father's approval but was not entirely to my taste.

Usually sick children attended the morning surgery with their mothers or with their grandmothers if their mother was avant garde enough to still be working shifts at Henleys or Bowaters. Old Nan was definitely not the kind of grandparent who had ever been known to exhibit enough care and concern for a grandchild to accompany them on a doctor's visit and in any case my own mother liked to be firmly in charge of health matters. She looked down on working women and called them Flighty because they were no better than they ought to have been and their minds were on silk stockings and lipsticks rather than their Poor Little Mites and some of them even Carried On with other women's husbands down in Crete Hall Road after their shifts ended. It was their poor husbands she felt sorry for because they were likely to be working their fingers to the bone and how were they being rewarded? That's what she would like to know. She thanked the Lord that at least she had never been one known for Carrying On.

As for the late afternoon surgery, that was largely attended by sick adults such as Mary Newberry regularly bent over with abdominal pain that was the bane of her life every month as regular as clockwork and men with the kind of cough that never quite went away despite changing to Players' Weights. At least half the patients smoked relentlessly to while away the lengthy waits for attention. From time to time a flurry of excitement would be caused when someone was brought in by a relative and clearly more in need of immediate medical help than those who waited patiently on the mismatched chairs. Then when the bell tinkled the person poised to rise from their place might virtuously announce in a voice intended for all to hear, that the sicker one should go ahead without delay on account of their need being greater. They were profusely thanked and the offer invariably taken up.

When this happened all the waiting women would sit up a little straighter and fold their arms and exchange glances one to another signalling disapproval. These pockets of malcontent were never directed towards he or she being rapidly ushered towards medical assistance, but rather they who had so charitably given up their place in the queue. General opinion dictated that the public spirited one should by rights take the turn of the sick newcomer and go to the end of the line. Nothing was actually said until the miscreant themselves headed towards the consulting room when a murmur of discontent would arise. It was all very well to give up your place, it was pointed out, but by rights you should then go right down the queue. When all was said and done there could be no argument. In fact there was no argument because one and all knew what was fair and those who did not perhaps entirely agree simply remained silent, sucked on the end of their Woodbines and stared into the middle distance.

The discontent triggered by this scenario was so predictable that it became uninteresting and I would rapidly turn my attention back to Birds of Prey and wonder if Hovering Kestrel was in fact preferable to Falcon in Flight. Years later my brother who was so drawn to all birds of prey whether or not they were British, said that he always enjoyed his visits to Outred's waiting room even when suffering severe ear ache and revealed to me that his love affair with the Kestrel that had begun with the stuffed bird in a glass dome in Great Aunt Martha's Station Road parlour, was firmly established by the local doctor's choice of waiting room wall decoration.

Later still when I found myself charged with the care of the exasperating bird temporarily housed in the spare bedroom of his Chatham semi-detached, my mind strayed back to those Birds of Prey prints. I took comfort from the fact that had it been The Glorious Golden Eagle rather than Hovering Kestrel that ultimately met with the overall approval of my ever more fanatical sibling this period of guardianship might have been a great deal more challenging. But that of course is another story.

The Very First Paddyfield Warbler

In the early 1950s we were not aware that the desolate North Kent marshland just a hop, skip and a jump from our York Road terraced house, and stretching from Dartford in the west to Whitstable in the east, would in the not too distant future be recognized as one of the most important natural wetlands in Northern Europe. Nevertheless my ornithology-obsessed young brother always seemed to have known that up to 300,000 migrant birds used the Thames mudflats as a regular stop-off point in their routine journeys between the Arctic and Africa. The Estuary marshland is now one of more than twenty environmentally sensitive areas recognized by the Department for the Environment, Food and Rural Affairs now known as DEFRA. In more recent years the Royal Society for the Protection of Birds has taken over considerable stretches of the Hoo Peninsula including Northward Hill, High Halstow and parts of Sheppey. Even the Medway Council's Riverside Park at Gillingham is an example of managed public access to the wetland but back then the area was largely uncontrolled. It became totally familiar to Bernard as he ventured ever further from home and deeper into the ambiguities of local wildlife.

He was not generally lacking in confidence as far as meandering away from York Road was concerned but there were definitely times when he would cajole me into accompanying him and this might have been more out of a desire to convert me to a particular enthusiasm rather than a lack of self-assurance. I recall ongoing trips over years to the greatly revered Rook Roost at Northward Hill necessitating interminable changes of buses and lengthy periods of walking. In time of course I began to regret that very first visit we made and my assurance that we could return at any stage. Little wonder perhaps that I displayed somewhat less apathy when he first mentioned the Paddyfield Warbler he was quite certain he had discovered in reed beds where Swanscombe merged into Northfleet and should by rights be nominated as Ours. No changes of bus were needed, no complicated timetables to be studied. He urgently wanted me to return with him to see it and when I asked why it was so important he claimed it was a most unusual discovery because the Paddyfield Warbler was quite unknown in the area. I may have said something about him possibly being mistaken in that case but without a great deal of conviction because I knew from experience that where identification of birds was concerned he was invariably right.

For days he could speak of nothing else, bombarding me with details as to its likely wingspan – 15 to 17cm and possible weight – 8 to 13 gr and the fact that the example he was certain he had seen was definitely light brown in colour though with paler plumage beneath. At first he had thought it might simply be a Sedge Warbler, still exciting but hardly inconceivable but upon a second visit he became convinced that it was in fact the known to be elusive Paddyfield Warbler, not ever seen in this part of North Kent previously – at least as far as he was aware. At his insistence and in heavy rain we set forth to Swanscombe one Saturday afternoon and spent an uncomfortable hour or two awaiting the arrival of Our Bird back to the reed beds that should by rights have belonged to Northfleet.

Sister Joseph, head teacher at the school in Springhead Road, reported that he had been missing for over a week when he finally and triumphantly waved a series of blurred and out of focus photographs of the kind we referred to as Snaps back then in her face. She was singularly unimpressed. The thoroughly modern Kodak camera borrowed from Cousin Margaret's unknowingly generous young husband was returned intact and unscathed and the images that could have been clearer were shown to all and sundry who had ever shown an interest in local birdlife. The problem was that not a great deal of interest ensued.

It was a sad fact that my brother paid little attention to what was happening at school, feeling it was largely an imposition in his life. Having very little understanding of mathematics as he grew older he avoided attendance on days featuring that subject and so his understanding diminished even further. His interest in ornithology was already well established and he spent as much time as humanly possible wandering the marshes from Crayford to Higham indulging what had become a passion. By the time he was fourteen he had engaged in a great deal of deceit and petty crime in order to finance bus fares, bird books and the acquisition of a pair of binoculars that eventually resulted in a brush with the police. Old Nan who was engaged in a fair amount of petty crime herself said little about his minor thefts and the ongoing duplicity in his life but was vocal that the sooner he discarded that Tomfool Bird Business the better. He's to be a grown man in next to no time and it looked like he'd be one with a mania – It wasn't natural! My mother, who had unwittingly and somewhat surprisingly first inculcated the obsession by pointing out to him when he was two and three years old, thrushes in the hedgerow and the occasional chaffinch in the hawthorn bushes, was in despair. What had started as a pre-school diversion had developed into an overwhelming fixation. By the time he left school at just fifteen he had not distinguished himself academically in any way, preferring at all times not to catch the attention of the teaching staff. Largely he succeeded and emerged ready for the workforce with no practical skills.

It was our mother who noticed the card in the window of the New Road Butchery in Gravesend, announcing that a Boy was Needed. It was she who informed the prospective employer that she had just the Boy at home and in need of employment and that four pounds five shillings a week sounded very fair to her and that yes indeed he was a very keen lad, and most anxious for a future in butchery. But although he dutifully started the job and was even there on time each morning it was clear that his heart wasn't in it and quite apart from that the daily close proximity to raw flesh did nothing to inspire him. He began to talk to the butcher of the bird species that could be seen daily in the nearby marshland and acquainted him with the fact that once he had seen a Paddyfield Warbler, a rare variety but the trouble with that was that nobody really believed him. The butcher did not show a great deal of interest and so during his lunch break he spoke with those working in the Co-op just in case they proved to be more ornithologically aware than his employer but they turned out not to be. When a month or so passed and the butcher was beginning to wonder how he might best break the news to our mother that her keen son was not proving to be as eager for the job as he had hoped, Bernard decided that the only acceptable future for him was one spent living on the marsh in a pup tent of the kind first designed and used in the American Civil War. Also known as Shelter Halves, he had read of their simple construction, ease of assembly and the fact that as recently as WW2 they were still in use. A pup tent was definitely what he needed! He would erect it close to where he first saw the Paddyfield Warbler and with the aid of a butane gas device and a torch his future would be idyllic.

A splendid plan that paved the way for an immediate escape from years of butchery but unfortunately it was not going to be realized as rapidly as he had hoped. Neither pup tents nor primus stoves were quite as cheap as he had imagined them to be and might take as long as six weeks of hard saving. It was then that the germ of an idea that eventually involved the theft of the week's takings on its way to the bank was first devised. The degree of violence that ultimately accompanied the theft was not part of the original plan, of that he was adamant when persuaded to talk about the incident many years later.

Following this episode of undisputed criminal violence Bernard quite naturally panicked a great deal before making the much coveted purchase of tent and primus. He also bought a rather expensive torch, hiking boots and a great deal of chocolate before heading towards the point where Swanscombe mudflats joined the Botany Marsh at Northfleet. It was several days before the police finally found him there and he knew at once that he had probably been betrayed by his own mother.

    The Aunts were collectively shocked and talked in low voices about what had happened for months. Mag said it had been no surprise to her on account of Nell not having it in her to be much cop as a mother. She'd always been too hard on him – she was generally hard on both her kids if the truth be told. Sometimes it was necessary to know when to hold back and not give too many hidings. Nell handed out too many wallops and she was too inclined towards thick ears especially since her Bern had Gone. Martha said she thanked the Almighty that she only had her Pat and had never had to bring up a boy especially one like him with his mind stuffed full of Tomfool ideas but you had to admit that life wasn't easy for widows and she knew that only too well since the war took her Paddy. Maud, who still Thank God had her George, was glad her Desmond had been just that much older and not influenced by Nell's boy and at least he was at a different school because it was at school where most of the trouble started in her experience. Old Nan thought that too much was made of school and not having a day of it had done her no harm whatsoever. The problem with that boy was that he was bad through and through, though she wouldn't mind betting that it had been the school that had filled his head with all the bird tripe in the first place.

    Meanwhile our mother felt more inadequate than ever, attended the Juvenile Court Hearing, and tried to listen attentively to those who Knew Better than she as to what would become of her lawless son. The Children and Young Persons Act had recently raised the age of criminal responsibility to 10 but it had also required local authorities to undertake preventative work with families who had children at risk of re-offending. My brother was deemed to be at risk even before he was discovered cold and hungry in his new pup tent and so he progressed through the hands of a number of well-meaning officers assigned to him by the Court. It was discovered that the unfortunate butcher had not been his first victim as far as straightforward theft was concerned and that he had been responsible for various acts of pilfering ranging from raiding the purses and wallets of relatives when they came to visit, appropriating our mother's carefully saved Christmas fund from the top of her wardrobe, and helping himself to a number of LPs, purchases I had made in advance of owning a record player but hopeful that someday I would. These he sold in Gravesend Market. For some time he had not lacked energy and enthusiasm for delinquency on a small scale and it had undoubtedly been the single act of sudden violence that had propelled him towards a category more alarming and with infinitely more consequences.

The Probation Officer called Ken managed to get alongside Bernard and earn his trust sufficiently to ensure that from time to time he listened to the advice offered him. Ken organized a weekly amount of spending money and was hopeful of sorting out a place at the Gravesend School of Art until he realized it had merged with the Medway College. Bernard had of course revealed the well-thumbed photographs of the Paddyfield Warbler and Ken quite sensibly believed he might benefit from a course in photography which would not only cater to his innate creativity but it had nothing whatsoever to do with mathematics which was a bonus. Bernard was in agreement but cautious all the same because it sounded just a little like school in disguise and our mother was elated to be able to say that she had a son who would be attending College which was odd as she had shown little interest in Further Education for either of us previously. However, when the idea came to fruition and Bernard took the train to attend on a daily basis she was almost bursting with pride and told all and sundry that he went to a Proper College where the uniform was a cap and gown. In retrospect I think this odd idea must have filtered down via comic books from her youth featuring a mishmash amalgamation of Gem, Magnet and Greyfriars School. It also had something to do with the continuing censure and disapproval of her mother and sisters who voiced ongoing criticism of both Bernard's criminal behaviour and her own less than ideal parenting that had probably facilitated it.

The completion of the photography course and the skills acquired ensured that he would undoubtedly be in a much better position to produce first class images of the Paddyfield Warbler should the situation ever again present itself. At some stage I remember pointing that or something very similar, out to him. He seemed immediately dejected at the thought and said that no matter how hard he had tried he was never able to persuade anyone in the ornithology world that he had actually seen the bird. He was repeatedly told that it did not appear in the area and he had definitely been mistaken.

Decades elapsed before an account appeared in a number of Bird Watching Journals that for the very first time a Paddyfield Warbler had been observed on the North Kent Marshes. An astonishing event! Great excitement was caused. Bernard said it might have been unusual but it certainly wasn't the first time it had been seen. His had been the very first Paddyfield Warbler and he had photographic evidence of that!

Miss Sands and the Swan

Looking back on those largely halcyon days of memory at Wombwell Hall I no longer know if the staff member I have locked into recall as Miss Sands the Religious Education Teacher was actually Mrs Sands. I even spent some time searching through the various comments made on School Reports during my time there but she always designated herself as simply MLS. She may have been Margaret Louise or Mary Leonie or maybe something much more innovative. It's hard to know after so many years but what I do know is that throughout my time attending her classes and feeling that I benefited from her tutelage it was only in the final term that I shone in any way because it was then that I came top in the Spring Term Examination. It was the first and only time I had come top in anything at all, either before or since, so little wonder that it is committed to memory. I think Miss Sands was as surprised as I was.

Until that significant result her comments on my Reports had hovered around remarks noting that with added application I had done better recently or even that I had worked with interest at a particular time but once I unexpectedly excelled she noted that I had not merely worked hard but done extremely well as my final examination result attested. The sudden success was bewildering as far as I was concerned and I later sensibly came to assume that it had something to do with the more academic students having little interest in matters pertaining to religion whereas I could become quite engrossed in the idea of a Special Being and all the ideas both metaphysical and logical that accompanied such a presence. I had not at that time yet considered that God might be male or female, being altogether too engrossed in wondering if any particular idea or ideal connected to spirituality was in fact a force for good or evil in the world. You could argue either way and that's generally what I did if I couldn't find a real person to argue with. I blame Roman Catholicism because there is something about growing up within the Faith, even via a group of rather lapsed believers such as The Constants and The Hendys, that predisposes their young towards a general commitment and allegiance to the philosophy of One True God. And quite apart from that of course the Catholic Church has always been overly fond of sinners and basks in the glorious idea of Penitents. Little wonder that some bored teenagers such as myself toyed seriously with the idea of a life spent in a Nunnery.

Miss M.L Sands had an appearance that was as sandy as her name. Although she was not in any way overweight she always appeared bulky and seemed uncomfortable in her clothes. She wore plaid patterned skirts in various sandy shades and hand knitted cardigans with intricate patterns, one of which featured a swan on a beige background stretching from left to right across the shoulders as it paddled upon a lake. Miss Sands' knitwear was never made of ten ply QuikKnit yarn but always of four ply which as every knitter knew took forever to complete. For this reason my own Forest Green school cardigans were always without fail constructed from

QuikKnit purchased from a stall in the Saturday market because my mother was an inveterate and impatient knitter and greatly irritated by lack of progress. Once I learned to knit competently myself I was astonished at how unlikely it was for her to unpick even a line in order to retrieve a dropped stitch. Such irascibilities were definitely not a feature of the workmanship displayed by whoever created the collection of cardigans worn by Miss Sands in the early 1950s, however.

Julia Hill who had, until I excelled so surprisingly, usually gained the highest R.E. mark, had confidently been expected to do so once again. She was a great favourite with the sandy R.E. teacher and they were consequently rather appreciative of each other. Julia admired the Sea Island Cotton shirts worn under the four ply cardigans and the careful embroidery on the collars, featuring woodland flowers and from time to time the wearer's initials – MLS, beautifully sewn and displaying the effortless assurance of a confident stitcher. Julia, never known to lack confidence, said that had she not been playing Malvolio in the class drama production of Twelfth Night that term she would certainly not have allowed herself to be beaten by someone like me. I definitely did not like the way she said that but did not particularly wish to make a complete enemy of her so did not retaliate. Miss K Smith, she added, was a hard taskmaster where performance was concerned and when I feigned disinterest she looked at me knowingly and added that everyone was aware that I was wildly in love with Miss K.S and couldn't understand why I had not bothered to audition for a part myself. With three rehearsals weekly there would then have been no time left for useless and boring R.E.

exam swot. I ignored these remarks and continued to consider how unlikeable this particular classmate was.

Although I found the R.E. classes a great deal more interesting than mathematics or science or geography at times I thought some of the things Miss Sands said were hard to accept and she was most of the time disinclined to debate a point. On one occasion when she was talking about Simon Peter washing the feet of Jesus she hastily added that it had not been an act of humility or obeisance but simply because that's what people did in those days in that part of the world. It was hot and dusty and whereas we might wash our hands and face, Jesus and his Disciples would rather use any available water to wash their hot and dusty feet. It was a very sensible use of the water in fact. People did not waste water back then the way we were inclined to in the spring of 1956. I asked her if she was absolutely sure of that and she seemed quite annoyed and said of course she was sure. Jesus would have been one hundred per cent against Acts of Humility and Obeisance – he simply was not that kind of human being and that was totally clear. It wasn't altogether clear to me but I did not query this line of thought further.

Valerie Goldsack and her best friend Yvonne from Swanscombe told me they were amazed that the first time I came top in anything it happened to be R.E. because Miss Sands did not seem to like me all that much. I agreed that I had been quite startled myself but put it down to having a particular interest in religion which made them look at each other knowingly and exchange smiles before Valerie ventured that her father had said it was something of a Soft Subject, a bit like Anthropology was said to be for those going to University. It wasn't difficult, she said, to do well in R.E so I added that I was definitely considering devoting my life to God by becoming a nun which seemed to amuse them even more. Yvonne said that R.E. was the most boring class of the week in her opinion and she really disliked Thursday afternoons simply because of it except for the times when Miss Sands used Bad Language which could be hilarious. Valerie said that when she told her father about those shocking terms he checked out the details in their Home Encyclopedia because he had definitely not liked the sound of the expressions that had been bandied about.

 They were referring to the recent occasion when Miss Sands told us that the Ark of the Covenant and furniture of the Tabernacle were made of Shittim Wood. There had been sharp intakes of breath from girls like Valerie and Yvonne and perhaps also Julia and barely suppressed giggles from at least a third of the remainder. The rest of us looked at each other uncertainly and then watched with horror as Miss Sands began to write squeakily but firmly on the board in bold letters – Shittim Wood! After an interminable silence Julia asked in her Malvolio stage-projected voice if that particular wood had always had that name because she had never heard of it and then outbreaks of proper laughter erupted from various areas at the back of the room so she tossed her head and looked behind her, appreciatively and then sat up a little straighter. Julia Hill the Actress – Miss Hill the Entertainer! Miss Sands said in a voice that did not change in any way that it was the wood of the Shittah Tree now more commonly known as the Acacia. She carefully added the words Shittah and Acacia to the chalkboard. The various woods mentioned in the Bible were interesting, she told us. Some people, she added, seemed to think that Dogwood had been used for the cross on which Our Lord was crucified and that later the tree became ashamed so God ensured that it would henceforth grow small and twisted and never be used for such a purpose again. She added that according to the sacred tradition of the Eastern Orthodox Church the True Cross had been fashioned from three different varieties of wood – Cedar, Pine and Cypress. These varieties she carefully added to the list on the board. Then she looked directly at Rimma Klatz because her family was Russian and therefore she must surely have insider knowledge with regard to the Orthodox Church. In point of fact Rimma's family was Jewish and had fled from a village pogrom early in the twentieth century. They were possessed of little of the knowledge Miss Sands attributed to them. But that was hardly her fault as she couldn't be expected to know everything. I wondered how the mysterious Orthodox Church differed from the Church we were all reasonably familiar with but did not like to ask.

On R.E. afternoons I usually walked to the bus stop with Gloria Glover who was on the Shittim Wood occasion still highly amused by the incident that had brightened up the last class of the day. She said you could always rely on Religious Education to provide a few laughs and wasn't Miss Sands a card? I nodded doubtfully and a few weeks later when I wanted to discuss with her the fact that I had come top in the exam Gloria just said well somebody had to come top and it might as well be me if I was really serious about becoming a nun. I should know, she said, that if Julia Hill had wanted to, she could easily have beaten me because she was what all the staff called An Outstanding Student and Gloria had actually heard Miss K. Smith mention her Outstandingness one afternoon after Hockey to Miss S. Smith. I wondered if that was true but even if it wasn't I found the idea of Miss K. Smith saying such a thing strangely irritating.

Several months after I left Wombwell Hall I very nearly came face to face with Miss Sands the R.E. teacher in the Promenade Gardens, in Gravesend. She was accompanied by a woman who to all intents and purposes was simply an older version of herself, sandy and bulky and bent over, leaning heavily upon a stick. Perhaps it was her mother. She was in a heated altercation with a teenage boy from whom she appeared to have confiscated a catapult. He had attacked one of the swans, apparently, a fact that she had clearly found deeply distressing. I paused to see what might happen next, but far enough away from them not to be noticed. As the confrontation refused to descend into anything more excitingly violent, after a while I began to walk away – but not before I noticed that she was wearing her Four Ply cardigan with the paddling swan across the back. There was something strangely uplifting about that and for the briefest second or two I wanted to say Hello.

When Your Face Doesn't Fit

I had never heard of Ringing Permits until I was well into my teens. I didn't know that there were enthusiasts who spent a great deal of time putting tags or rings on birds for a variety of reasons and even when the reasons were explained to me at a later stage I couldn't really work up much enthusiasm for the idea. On the other hand my brother demonstrated a great deal of enthusiasm. For some time, and for the life of me I cannot now remember when the Ringing Permit preoccupation began, he was most anxious to become a member of the British Trust for Ornithology and be granted the required permission to put plastic identification tags onto the legs of birds. His uninformed and largely uninterested family couldn't see the attraction although as hobbies go it was relatively harmless and kept him nicely away from diversions that might well prove more damaging and possibly even shameful for the rest of us.

The only problem that seemed to emerge was, our mother said, as plain as the nose on your face and it was clearly down to his face not fitting. She said this once she learned that if you wanted to be welcomed into the particular fraternity that so attracted him it paid to be just a bit posh if you could manage it. No-one in their right mind would have described any member of our family as remotely posh so you could say a distinct disadvantage existed from the very start and it was never going to be easy. On the other hand what we lacked in poshness we perhaps made up for in determination.

The ringing scheme in Britain had started in 1909 and was really a combination of schemes, one instigated by a certain Harry Forbes Witherby and the other by Arthur Landsborough Thomson. A third scheme launched by Country Life Magazine also began around this time but WW1 intervened and by the 1930s all these systems had morphed onto one – the British Trust for Ornithology known by those familiar with it as simply the BTO.

In its earliest years it seems that the BTO pioneers simply set out to find answers to some of the most basic questions of the time. Where did those birds arriving in summer actually spend the winter? Where did the winter visitors spend the summer? Where did they breed? Back in the earliest days of these studies, even the migration routes were only realised from observations of groups preparing for journeys in spring and autumn and at one time there was even a suggestion that swallows spent their winters at the bottom of ponds. My Grandmother for one firmly believed that or claimed that she did. From her point of view it seemed a likely alternative to the far-fetched idea that they would embark upon a journey of thousands of miles. Apparently the first recovery of a ringed swallow came in December 1912 as far away as South Africa. This caused astonishment to Harry Witherby reporting in *British Birds, Volume 6* who noted that it seemed to him quite extraordinary that a bird that bred in the far west of Europe should have somehow reached the South-East of Africa. Information gathering regarding swallows and where they spent their winters henceforth became a trendy pastime that attracted the middle classes and those emulating them.

Bernard was certainly captivated by these awe-inspiring avian journeys and became ever more determined to join the ranks of those considered trustworthy and responsible enough to document them for the purposes of posterity via the possession of a Ringing Permit. But achieving that goal took much longer than he could have possibly anticipated on account of his face not fitting. He thought it might be to do with the fact that the efficient funding of the organisation relied upon donations from prominent citizens in various areas and as he grew older he was fearful that those in and around the Thames Estuary might well be too familiar with his unhappy history as a Gravesend butcher's assistant and the rapid termination of that employment. Securing an early record for what was then termed Robbery with Violence did little to enhance anyone's reputation and was an abomination as far as many of the Good and the Great of Gravesend were concerned. It was a definite problem that at that particular time a cluster of them were avid bird enthusiasts. All very unfortunate.

Our grandmother did not endear herself to any of us by pointing out that being somewhat Light Fingered in general did not help matters when it came to creating a good impression with Toffs. As she was undoubtedly Light Fingered herself this observation was never likely to be received well and my mother steadfastly insisted that it was more to do with having a face that didn't fit than anything else and what's more you could never really tell in advance how your face was likely to be received. Luckily as time went on things changed and bird ringing became less the province of the middle classes and eventually presented in many guises from individuals in urban areas to large groups over a wide geographic area. It was no longer quite as necessary to make absolutely certain that you had a spotless reputation. Ages eventually ranged from under ten to over eighty and of course in due course the much coveted Permit was to be granted despite the fact that the earlier transgressions did not simply disappear and the reported habit of light fingeredness definitely remained.

Bernard saturated himself in more and more stories of awe-inspiring migrations and even as recently as 2015 told me in some excitement that a Sand Martin ringed at a Hampshire colony was re-captured by the very same ringer the next winter in Morocco! These remarkable recoveries graphically illustrated impressive and regular journeys that for the truly addicted are hard to overlook although for the uninitiated sometimes the detail is difficult to truly appreciate. I still struggle to understand why it was so unpredictable that an Arctic Tern should fly into a Japanese whaler off Antarctic pack ice thus finding notoriety as the only BTO ringed bird to be found at a Southern latitude higher than the Northern latitude at which it was ringed. Why should it not do so if it so chose?

I learned these facts bit by bit over time whether I wanted to or not because every conversation with my brother over at least two decades was peppered with them. I was told that as the ringing scheme itself grew in size and in age then so did the recorded ages of the focus of its very existence. Apparently very few wild birds reach anything like their potential age simply because too many factors work against them. They deal with not only accidents and predators but weather, disease, starvation and old fashioned bad luck. This came as no surprise to our various aunts who were regularly also privy to this particular monologue. It was their opinion that birds were a bit like the rest of us because we could all do with a bit more good luck. That aside, some of the longevities seemed quite staggering. A Manx Shearwater had apparently recorded an age of 51 years, a Razorbill 42 years, an Oystercatcher 40 years and a Pink-footed Goose 39 years. These records seemed even more remarkable when the vast distances covered in their lifetimes were considered. The Manx Shearwater from Wales would have spent all of 51 winters off the coast of Argentina thus covering 1.5 million kilometres just travelling to and fro.

Although Bernard quickly realised that the ringing process was carried out by those with skill who had the utmost consideration for the welfare of their feathered friends he quickly became a vocal opponent of the most frequently used method, the mist net. These were erected between poles and designed to catch birds in flight. It was apparent that their removal could only be safely effected by the most experienced ringers. The problem seemed to be that from time to time the procedure resulted in the death of many birds and he was thus far more attracted to the idea of ringing chicks in the nest and justified this standpoint by saying that at least the precise age and origins was then known.

In spite of the fact that his views did not always win him friends he served an elongated apprenticeship under the close supervision of others and eventually learned the essential abilities that involved the safe and efficient catching and handling of birds, the identification, ageing, measuring and record keeping. The only setback seemed to be that on each occasion that his permit needed to be renewed there was invariably rather more delay in the process than he felt was usual or necessary. Our mother shook her head knowingly on every occasion this happened, bent over the current piece of knitting she was involved in and said she had told him over and over again it was on account of his particular face and that was a fact no matter how reliably he turned up at 5 am on the North Kent Marshes.

It was certainly another fact that Bernard had always been drawn to the Northfleet and Gravesend marshland and throughout his ringing period had assiduously progressed through the study of a variety of Estuary migrants together with tits and finches on bitter cold winter mornings. During the breeding season of warblers he was reliably on site at least thirty minutes before those whose faces had always fitted. His conscientious attentiveness eventually paid off and when he suggested that he was more than anxious to make the leap to owl chicks in nest boxes and hawks of every persuasion after some discussion he was allowed to do so. He began to think that perhaps in time he would even have the good fortune to tag a Golden Eagle.

I was definitely aware of his ambition regarding the Golden Eagle. I knew that from the time he first became aware of its existence he had nursed a desire to become more acquainted with it. I fully understood that it was the Golden Eagle that drew him so frequently to the North of Scotland and that eventually became the prime reason for him making his home there in the last ten years of his life.

His wife on the other hand, uprooted from the comfort of the Kentish village surrounded by friends and family, took longer to come to terms with it and called it a Fixation. It was clear that pleasing everyone was impossible.

A Bird Called Kairo

It didn't occur to me to question where the bird came from, not back then at the turn of the 1970s. I was the very opposite of curious yet I knew it was improbable that it had been found in the average pet shop. It would have even been unlikely to happen upon one in that extraordinary Pet Department that once nestled in the far corner of the fourth floor of Harrods where I once bought a hamster that inexplicably perished on the way home. They of course gave us our money back. You could get all manner of odd creatures at Harrods. It was rumoured that in 1933 Noel Coward bought an alligator there to surprise a friend for Christmas and as recently as 1967 it had been possible to purchase a lion cub. But there were no Kestrels as far as I recall and possibly that was because they simply weren't popular. I could certainly understand that.

The bird I now refer to had been given the name Cairo for some reason now long forgotten and Cairo with a K rather than a C – Kairo. Now I begin to think about it the most likely reason for Bernard's possession of it was that he filched it from the nest among Alice the Falconer's window boxes. He certainly would not have bothered seeking the permission of those with Authority even had he had been required to because his desire to possess one became overwhelming. At times I wondered why this was because it was he who told me that the bird had for hundreds of years occupied a lowly status in falconry and in the middle ages was spoken of derisively as the Knave. In the late 1960s the Barry Hines novel about Billy Caspar in his cheerless Northern town finding and training such a bird inspired him further and he read and re-read the book, becoming even more glued to Ken Loach's film a year or so later. He began to refer to the Kestrel in a strangely soft voice by its old country name of Windhover – therefore, as I said, Kairo's appearance in his life was not altogether unexpected.

I was with him when he first met Alice in her 20th floor council flat somewhere in South London and I was only there because his wife-at-the-time, Janice, refused to go with him despite the fact he had been voluble to me and my partner-at-the-time, Vidar, about Janice being his Best Friend and that he simply would not be able to cope with life without her. Janice said that kind of talk was always a bad sign. Someone, she pointed out sensibly, had to stay home in the flat above the Painting & Decorating Store in Camden Passage and look after the baby. She was absolutely not prepared to subject the child to yet another jaunt into the further reaches of suburbia in search of strange and anomalous species. Vidar had expressed a similar lack of interest so that's how it came that just the two of us climbed twenty flights of stairs because the lift was not functioning on an unusually chilly late May evening.

Alice was a small bird-like woman herself, in her sixties with tightly permed hair and a husband in a wheelchair due to a long-ago accident in a swimming pool. She was waiting for the Council to rehouse her or, alternatively, ensure that the lift could be relied upon because the top floor was not what anyone would call convenient for wheelchair living though it did of course have a splendid view. She told us that it was the third year in a row that the birds had raised a family in her window boxes and she'd never heard of Kestrels. When Bernard spoke of falcons and hawks and birds of prey she looked alarmed and wondered if the cat was safe with them though they'd shown little interest in it so far. That year there were five chicks for them to care for and she had felt concerned for them and even offered them budgie seed which they did not seem to like so she was trying them on bread soaked in warm milk but they'd turned out to be fussy eaters. Bernard looked horrified at the described diet and spoke of the importance of trying to maintain their natural diet of voles or mice or bats or shrews and failing these culinary favourites, perhaps worms and insects. Alice looked equally aghast and blinked rapidly whilst the husband in the wheelchair turned up the volume on the television and said feeding wild birds was a damn fool idea if ever he'd heard one and if they wanted bread and milk they'd make bloody sure they knew what time the milkman drove past.

The objects of the discourse meanwhile, hunched in their home among the petunias and geraniums interspersed with the mint for the Sunday roast, looked guarded, wary and later Bernard said it was more than likely because they were expecting yet another onslaught of indigestible budgie seed. I could not help noticing that he looked a little cautious himself as he bent to examine them and there was just the slightest suggestion of a tremor in his hands. He was talking about falcons being smaller birds than hawks and that they killed their prey quite differently and how to tell the female from the male. The male, he whispered, was the one with the blueish greyish head and the female was the bigger one, the one that was a bit browner. The male had bright yellow legs and feet – could I see that? I couldn't but I agreed that I could. When I whispered back that I had never seen one before he reminded me that Little Nanny of Hamerton Road had surely had a stuffed one under a glass dome in her parlour and did I not remember that? In any case he said, they were widespread throughout the country except perhaps on Shetland where there were no voles. Were there voles in South London I wondered but he seemed to think that didn't matter particularly because voles were not absolutely vital – they would easily take to sparrows if needs be. There was a lot of goodness in a sparrow from a kestrel's point of view.

Somehow it happened that a day or two later we went back to Alice's flat with a reporter and photographer from the local newspaper and had our photos taken alongside Alice and the birds that the following week appeared under the headline Alice of Crompton Court – Falconer Extraordinaire! She definitely thought that the publicity might help with the problem of the non-functioning lift and perhaps it did because I don't remember having to face the twenty flights after that though I know we visited Alice on frequent occasions during that early summer.

It was a few years after his acquaintance with a complete family of falcons that Bernard made an odd request of me that I was at first reluctant to agree to. Would I be prepared to stay at his new home in Chatham, Kent to take care of a pet bird and his small son whilst he and his wife spent a few days in Scotland in search of eagles? I had a small son of my own at this stage and thought it might be fun for the children to spend time together and a pet bird was not going to be too much trouble so with still some doubts I agreed. I think I might have envisaged something diminutive in a cage. I was definitely not expecting Kairo and was dismayed to find that the bird lived in the spare room adjacent to the kitchen, on a perch arrangement to which it was tethered. Even more alarming was the fact that I was expected to perform care rituals such as Loosening the Jesses and offering portions of food that absolutely must be as fresh as possible and have a measure of roughage attached.

For my convenience a dead mouse had already been dissected into Kestrel sized pieces and was in the fridge beside the left over chicken. Before I even made the query I was sternly advised that the chicken was not also destined for the bird because Kestrels are not keen on cooked food – the chicken was for me and the children. If I could also manage to fly the bird I should not be surprised if it managed to catch something it particularly fancied. It was apparently inordinately fond of bats. In the interim when Kairo finished the mouse in the fridge I could cut up a wild rabbit, it was suggested because they were suicidal thereabouts and easy to run down at night in the headlights of the mini-van – and if I did so, to definitely not discard the fur. I said nothing though my heart was becoming heavy.

I would have been more than willing to give the creature a chance because it wasn't as if I was entirely against wildlife per se but it seemed to display an immediate resentment of me and scowled in so threatening a manner that I knew without question that our relationship was not going to be easy. Patrick, then aged about three, was cautiously asking his older cousin where the actual pet bird was. Not, he qualified, the angry looking one tied up on the ledge but the pet bird we were going to look after. The one, he added hopefully, that would be in a cage and Merlin, completely accustomed to all that the avian world could possibly produce within the confines of a small terrace house in Chatham, obligingly explained the situation. He clarified knowledgeably for one who had not yet reached school attendance age that falcons were never caged and the only ones he was familiar with lived on ledges to which they were attached just as Kairo was at that very moment.

And so Bernard and Janice left I felt in a somewhat hurried manner in search of eagles. With the children at a safe distance in the doorway of the spare room I scrutinized the bird and tried to recall the detailed instructions as to how the falconer's glove was to be used. I knew without doubt that things would ultimately go wrong. It was though a day or two before the situation completely deteriorated and during that time we three had proffered regular bits of raw mouse with the aid of kitchen tongs and congratulated ourselves when the offerings were rapidly consumed by the bird. The acceptance of the food might have been what gave me a false sense of security, a boost in confidence. I too might become a falconer and in any case why would I be afraid of a mere bird? Alice of Crompton Court after all had seemed quite at ease with her regular window box guests.

The problems began when somehow or other the bird got loose and although I tried diligently I could not persuade it to return to the ledge where it had originally been tethered. I've forgotten the details of how the calamity occurred but occur it did and no amount of tasty mouse morsels were going to lure it back to where our Chatham acquaintance began and I was led a merry dance throughout the small house, from kitchen to bathroom to bedroom and back again. Followed by the excited pre-schoolers I pursued it relentlessly attempting to bribe it with promises of raw bat just as soon as I could locate one. I consulted the various books on wild birds that proliferated the bookshelves because this of course was long, long before the advent of Google but nothing would persuade it to behave with anything like decorum.

In despair and during a hot chocolate break I gently enquired of my small nephew what his father might do at this stage should he find himself quite unable to catch a reprobate bird of prey. After a long pause he indicated he had no idea because to his knowledge such a thing had never happened and Kairo was a model of good behaviour with his father. He added helpfully that he had once seen his grandmother throw a teacloth over her budgie when it misbehaved so it would think it was night and go to sleep. It would indeed be wonderful if Kairo could be persuaded to sleep. With determination we began to throw tea-cloths but this activity was viewed with antagonism and the bird simply became more hyperactive. A few moments later when he perched precariously on the frame of a montage of family weddings sending them crashing onto the stairs he vengefully seemed to regard this as entirely our fault and withdrew once more to the kitchen where storage jars marked Rice and Vermicelli were also heard to clatter from their rightful place. So we abandoned the teacloth idea though Merlin assured me it had worked with Cheeky the Budgie.

I'm now unsure when it was I rang the local police station in despair – was it after two days of the Loose Kestrel or simply one? The constable on Desk Duty was quite matter-of-fact and called Dave. Kestrel-on-the-loose was it? Contrary creatures Kestrels could be. As it happened he was a bird man himself and even fancied himself as a bit-of-a-falconer so when he finished his shift he would be happy to pop round and see if he could help. Pop round he did, all burly reassuring six feet four inches of him. And once he donned the falconer's glove, Kairo seemed to suddenly tire of the game that had so tormented me and swooped down from his temporary perch on the topmost bookshelf atop of *British Birds of Prey* and settled upon it. Dave worked wonders with the jesses, speaking softly to the creature and advising me that I would be wise to keep a better eye on him but if I had any more trouble I should not hesitate to call him again.

Of course there is no need to elaborate on how delighted I was by the return of the eagle hunters the following evening. I didn't tell them the full story about Dave of course but mentioned that Kairo was probably homesick for the top floor flats at Crompton Court if in fact that had been his birthplace. For some reason he had not seemed completely happy or enjoy life the way a Kestrel should in the spare bedroom. Bernard was talking about eagles and absently stroking a wing feather I had not noticed on the kitchen floor but of course I wasn't listening – I could not wait to return to London!

Years later when my brother had long since moved on to his second-wife-Irene and my small nephew had long grown to manhood and probably forgotten all about the time in Chatham when three of us engaged in an extraordinary Kestrel hunt, I happened to read a most interesting wildlife article. It concerned the sudden and odd change of breeding habit that had seen Kairo and his antecedents of several years develop a proclivity for high rise Council flats living. The writer thought it possible that Alice's first pair had simply mistaken her window box at Crompton Court for a more convenient and customary clifftop. And possibly that is what happened.

Sid Strong & Ducks in Flight

Gravesend Borough Market received its charter in 1268 and is in fact one of the oldest markets in the country. My mother said rather vaguely that it had been there since the year dot and Old Nan agreed because it was definitely donkeys' years ago that somebody had the good sense to set it up. I can't say that I thought very much about the age of the place at the time of our many and regular visits there but later on when I came to realise that the construction of the Grand Bazaar in Istanbul did not begin until 1455 I retrospectively began to see it in better context. Not that I would ever suggest that the two markets could possibly be compared but it did make me stop and think about market charters which I hadn't ever done previously.

We made a trip there most Saturdays and I always looked forward to it even if one or two of the aunts and my grandmother came with us. We would set off on the bus during the mid-morning and first of all embark upon a tour of the shops in New Road and a lot of time would be spent admiring what was in the butcher's window and my mother might even make a purchase of half a dozen pork sausages. Aunt Mag was likely to dither a great deal and say she'd done all her Sunday dinner shopping already which remark might well result in Words between her and the sausage buyer because did she really believe that we were having sausages for our Sunday dinner? Could sausages, even the best pork ones, ever be described as a Sunday Roast? And later my mother would ruminate about the cheek of it especially since that saucy mare had finally made up her mind and gone in and bought a really lovely leg of lamb – having said she'd got all her Sunday shopping in! You wouldn't credit it really would you? But then you never got the truth of any matter out of Mag and she was well-known for saying one thing and meaning another.

The frostiness might even last through the cups of tea and biscuits from the café that used to be near the old Woolworths building but by the time we got to the market family relationships were usually back on an even keel again. The stall I was most interested in featured only second-hand books and was in the covered area just through and immediately beyond the bold, curving pediment upon which the date of the charter is given – 1268. That's when Henry III granted the Manor of Parrock the right to hold a Saturday market and an annual fair. For years I believed this to be the original structure and was annoyed to find that it was erected in 1898 and replaced an earlier building because I wondered what the earlier building had been like. The rest of the family were uninterested in books so I was usually left at this point to browse alone after my grandmother had loudly warned that I'd go blind with all that damn fool reading. I was usually allowed twenty minutes whilst the fabrics and bric-a-brac were examined and debated and food items such as live eels possibly purchased by Old Nan and then placed to thresh around in the bottom of her mock leather bucket bag or sometimes, more alarmingly, in the bottom of a string bag.

We barely gave the east end of the market more than a cursory glance, and the Grade II Listed figure of Queen Victoria was largely ignored because invariably we had little interest in proceeding into Queen Street on a Saturday. Always the Saturday visits terminated in Market Square where immediately to our right we would find Strong's Fancy Goods Ltd where the inimitable Sidney Strong the totally matchless market trader sold a wide range of china and glassware from the back of his lorry, aided by Young Gerald. Old Nan said that Young Gerald was his son and she knew that for sure because she'd been told by a cousin of Tubby Isaacs of Petticoat Lane fame. That was most probably not true because she was not someone who set a great deal of store by truth and I had to wonder if that's where I got it from because there were times when my own habit of habitually lying troubled me. Anyhow Sid himself maintained that Gerald was his younger brother. A few years later when I had become a fully-fledged teenager and ran away from home I came across Strong's Fancy Goods in Petticoat Lane myself and entered into conversation with Sid who tried to persuade me to return home. When I elected not to take his advice he took me with him on his weekly trip to buy china from manufacturers in Stoke-on-Trent. Later he drove me back to York Road and firmly deposited me on my home doorstep telling me I had a duty to my poor mother who must be worried to death and he would be if I was his. At some stage during the trip the question about his relationship with Young Gerald was raised, in all likelihood by me and I was told unequivocally that Gerald was his youngest brother and he was sick to death of being asked that question.

Back in the 1950s there was no real way of knowing the family relationships of market traders you had a passing Saturday acquaintance with for sure although for some reason we were all fascinated where the Strongs were concerned. However, all extraneous debate ceased once Strongy began to sell, launching with a great deal of energy into his familiar patter. Then the usual group of onlookers would gather at once, a large number of them not there to buy but simply as an admiring audience gathered shoulder to shoulder in anticipation whatever the weather.

There was no doubt that Strongy could hold the attention of a crowd, from the pre-schoolers in push chairs to the elderly leaning on their bamboo canes. Old Nan, generally more prone to criticism of salesmen rather than praise, admitted he was an Artiste and he should be on the bleeding stage and that was a fact. She'd certainly seen far worse at Collins Music Hall years ago and had to pay for the pleasure what's more. Meanwhile Strongy, seemingly oblivious to his entertainment value, expertly tossed an entire dinner set into the air and caught it again without as much as a resultant crack in a side plate and beamed around at the spectators delighting in the intakes of breath and spontaneous bursts of applause. It was at this point with an appreciative crowd in the palm of his hand that his patter would become his spiel, and pulling himself to his not inconsiderable full height it would rapidly morph into a kind of patois between himself and Gerald that he knew with satisfaction we would not understand a word of.

Although china was the main feature of his regular stock base in fact a wide range of other household goods reliably surfaced from the depths of the truck and at one time or another almost everyone you spoke to had made an important purchase from the Strongs. My grandmother was adamant that she had been a regular customer at their Sunday pitch in Petticoat Lane for years and particular buys in the past had been what she indelicately described as really lovely china Piss-pots, each one a work of art and that was a fact. Certainly each one of the many Constant daughters had been presented with one of these then essential items on the occasion of their weddings from Mag in the twenties right up to August 1939 when my mother was the last to walk down the aisle. Nobody expected Freda, the baby of the family, to ever find a husband because of her multiple personality problems and tendency to petty crime so somehow or other she was never counted as part of the marriage stakes. Lovely pieces of work those chamber pots had been though and Old Nan frequently reminded us that you just didn't see Piss-pots like that these days with all the new-fangled Bakelite and plastic. For one thing there was no weight in them and you didn't seem to get the same kind of decoration around the sides now did you? The one she gave Nell and Bern at the very advent of World War Two had been dusky pink and had been adorned with little golden cherubs flying alongside white doves. My mother was never amused when this story was repeated and when the giver was out of earshot said that if the truth be known she had been ashamed to receive such a gift but at the time had no option but to join in the laughter and put up with all the smutty jokes that went hand in hand with weddings. Her honest opinion was thank the Lord for plastic and long may it last.

The fact that Sidney Strong made regular appearances in Petticoat Lane on Sundays was at one time something of a surprise to us because we definitely saw him as belonging totally to Gravesend and of course our loyalty was first and foremost to our local market but as Aunt Martha pointed out, he had to make a living the same as the rest of us didn't he? And some market men were able to make a very good living by anyone's standards if former stall holder Alan Sugar is anything to go by. Perhaps Strongy never quite reached Sugar's dizzy heights but over the years it was obvious that all things considered he certainly wasn't on his uppers. In 1956 when he was seen at Meopham Green in The Cricketers my car-conscious cousin Harold couldn't help noticing that he seemed to have bought himself a brand-new Ford Fairlane and such a vehicle he pointed out would have set him back a bob or two and no mistake.

Certainly Strong's Fancy Goods basic stock became more diverse as time went on and aptly accommodated the household needs of the local clientele. There were dinner sets and canteens of cutlery for the newly-weds together with bedlinen and towels, followed by pushchairs and baby baths a year later in time for the first infants and by the mid-1950s glamorous items like electric blankets or even tea-making machines to be ostentatiously purchased by young marrieds like my cousin Margaret who was said to have more money than good sense.

Listening to Strongy launch into his sales patter was mesmerizing because it wasn't just a matter of raising an arm and saying that you would have one of them there electric blankets for two pounds ten shillings before they all went, or even determinedly waving the required sum at the seller. Strongy was absolutely not going to let his beloved blankets go that easily and he always elected not to take your money immediately because strangely he preferred to slash the price to two pounds, then astonishingly to one pound ten shillings. He was just giving them away at thirty bob and that was a fact. But then again – No he'd rather be robbed than take thirty bob from you and they would have to go at a guinea a piece! By this stage anticipation was high and instead of selling two blankets he'd be selling ten then twenty and be quickly down to the very last one. And who would take the last one off his hands? Then invariably if someone elected to do so he would find another last one in the back of the truck for the disconsolate and disappointed few fearful of remaining blanket-less.

And within this odd post-war mixture of hyped selling and East End humour Sid Strong briskly and proficiently sold a wide variety of domestic essentials to the families of Gravesend and Northfleet at prices to suit every pocket. There was no doubt whatsoever that he was indeed an Artiste if ever there was one and even my mother agreed with that. My grandmother said he put her in mind of Gus Elen years ago at the old Hackney Empire. He'd been known as the Coster Comedian and famous for ditties such as *Wait Until The Work Comes Around* that made you fall off your seat laughing. Gus Elen was always far superior to Harry Champion for instance in her opinion – but Old Strongy of Gravesend Market was one out of the bag though he never went in for singing of course. And it was for all these reasons together with items such as alarm clocks and toasters that the Saturday visits to the Market Square were a regular outing for so many members of the

Constant family as of course they were to hundreds of other families in the district.

One particular Saturday trip had been organised by the collective of aunts to celebrate a significant birthday for their mother and a fish and chip tea was going to be part of the treat, possibly even at The Reliance Fish Rooms, but before that could happen a visit to Strong's Fancy Goods was critical. My grandmother had expressed a great desire to own a group of china ducks to fly above the mantelpiece of the house in Iron Mill Lane, Crayford and she had been reliably informed that Strongy had a batch of them, suitable in every way, groups of three soaring skyward above a lake. My mother said as far as she was concerned she wouldn't give china ducks house room and they were definitely not worth the money you had to fork out for them but if that's what Mum wanted that's what Mum would get because there was no arguing with her once she got the bit between her teeth.

We waited patiently through the Finest Porcelain tea sets, sherry glasses packaged in neat half dozens, turquoise or navy if you fancied it candlewick bedspreads, easily mistaken for genuine tiger skin rugs, baby-bath-and-potty sets in pink or blue, shopping trolleys on wheels and walkie-talkie dolls with blonde brushable hair and at long last just when Old Nan's feet were killing her and her legs threatened to hold her no longer the ducks in flight that were easily attached to any wall, appeared. And as with everything else when Strongy first demanded thirty bob apiece we knew without doubt that within five minutes that sum would be reduced to twelve and sixpence much to everyone's pleasure and approval.

Later on as she sat upright and straight as ever over her halibut with extra chips and a liberal sprinkling of best vinegar my grandmother rather uncharacteristically said it was most definitely a blinder of a birthday celebration. She was glad she'd worn her coat with the fake fur collar because as birthdays go she hadn't had a better one since the time her Edgar, God rest his soul, took her to Brighton and they were thrown out of The Grand though for the life of her she couldn't remember how or why that happened.

It must have been all of fifteen years later when one of my cousins drew my attention to the fact that Strong's Fancy Goods Ltd had been very much in the news and in fact the talents of the incomparable Sid had at long last been recognised with him winning a silver cup and voted the best market auctioneer in Europe. Photos of Sid in Amsterdam holding his cup and looking very dapper in a silk mohair suit of the type later seen on the Kray Twins during their trial at The Old Bailey, had been in all the papers and what's more he had appeared on television to say a few words. My mother told me he'd said more than a few of course because he definitely had the gift of the gab but then again nobody minded because he'd always been a good sort and no wonder he'd done well. And did I remember the time he brought me back when I ran away, driving miles out of his way? And what about them lovely ducks we'd bought from him years ago for Old Nan that she still had flying over the fireplace. Not a mark on them and good as new because they were real quality. It had to be admitted that the Strongs only sold quality items – they were known for it. My brother, sitting at the kitchen table and idly turning the pages of a magazine called *Wildlife* murmured that if you looked at them properly you would see that they were not actually ducks of course – they were Canada Geese, but we ignored him.

Recalling Bluebirds

I was saddened enough to shed a few tears when Vera Lynn finally shuffled off her mortal coil at the great age of 103! Though I hadn't thought about her for years and if I had given her a passing thought I would have no doubt imagined that she died twenty years ago or more. That's what happens when you live in the antipodes because like it or not you become quite divorced from the trivia of those procedures and practices that ensure you never forget the enormous contribution wartime entertainers made to raise the hopes of the nation. And it's not simply ensuring that the memory is kept alive is it, because if you're anything like me you feel affronted to find that you simply don't know what is being referred to when some clever dick visiting from London decides they'll have a Vera at a local bar. On the other hand a Vera & Tonic doesn't exactly roll off the tongue does it? Neither does a Vera & Lemon. A Vera & Lime is less troublesome if you use care when tossing it into the banter.

Whether or not I had given her much thought during the intervening years there was no doubt at all that Dame Vera had featured very large indeed in my early childhood. For one thing her wartime repertoire was not only regularly played on the wireless but the refrains were echoed in-between the programming schedules by my mother. This wasn't as unfortunate as it sounds because back then not only did mothers sing on a daily basis as a matter of course but mine had a very good singing voice that she enjoyed showing off to the neighbours. Singing accompanied hanging out the washing, beating the rugs, doing the ironing and chopping vegetables for a healthy Ministry of Food suggested wartime stew. Consequently the popular catalogue of Vera Lynn melodies had by 1944 become part of me and I was lyric perfect in *We'll Meet Again, The White Cliffs of Dover, A Nightingale Sang in Berkeley Square, It's a Lovely Day Tomorrow*, and many more besides.

To some extent the hits of the 1940s supplanted and displaced my earlier repertoire learned from my Grandmother – *Two Lovely Black Eyes, Down at the Old Bull & Bush, Boiled Beef & Carrots* and *The Boy I Love is up in the Gallery*. Old Nan herself maintained she never thought that much of Vera Lynn and when all was said and done she wasn't a patch on Florrie Forde or Marie Lloyd. The Aunts as one though asserted, when she was safely out of earshot, that was because Edgar Constant, their late father had harboured a very sweet spot for Vera, never missing her regular 15 minute broadcasts and saying she brought a tear to his eye. His penchant for the young songstress had been something of a bone of contention between them because my grandmother was never good at sharing attention.

My own overall wartime favourite was *The White Cliffs of Dover* because when it came to the line about Jimmy going to sleep in his own little room again my mother always unseated poor Jimmy, replacing him with Jeannie. By the time of the Normandy Landings I had become convinced that the song had been written especially with me in mind. The only area of confusion lay with the Bluebirds and this was because I had never actually seen one in real life. When I asked about it I was simply told that it was a dear little bird, all blue in colour and shaped a bit like a Robin Redbreast and what's more when you saw one it made you feel warm and happy. I began to form the opinion that the bluebird was generally perceived as a symbol of joy and an expectation of everlasting happiness. To see the flocks of them that were anticipated over Dover's white cliffs would surely mean that nothing too awful was ever likely to happen again. It was to be years before I realized that although I was generally spot-on in my bluebird analysis, I was unlikely to light upon one easily as they lived mostly in North America as did the song's composer and lyricist – Walter Kent and Nat Burton. Perhaps the pair simply believed that their ubiquitous local bird was global or perhaps, more obscurely, it was an allusion to the American pilots as apparently the allied planes had their undersides painted sky-blue for some reason to do with camouflage.

So although the bluebird remained a bit of a mystery, the other bird that back then pre-occupied Dame Vera – the nightingale, certainly did not. Old Nan said that although she didn't think she'd ever laid eyes on one, what with them saving their songs for after dark, you certainly heard them often enough and not just in Berkeley Square either which was a place she did not normally frequent. She'd heard them at Cliffe Woods, and again in Cobham Village and once as large as life one night in Iron Mill Lane, Crayford she'd swear it. And then my mother would tell of the time she and my father heard one on Blackheath while waiting for a bus. Aunt Mag might then ask if she'd heard from her Bern recently and how was he but not much would be said further because the fact that Mag's Harold had not been Called Up on account of what was said to be vital war work was a sensitive issue

News of my father was of little interest to me back then because I had only the very vaguest memory of him although I had to blow a kiss to his photograph every evening on my way to bed and I knew that he had bought me my teddy bear prior to leaving to join the Eighth Army. Now he was apparently fighting the enemy in some foreign place where the food was said to be shocking and I was doubtful that he would ever bother to return so I gave him little thought. There were other complications to emerge eventually to do with his time serving in places like Italy and North Africa that were to cause considerable distress but I was always somehow too young for them to directly disturb my overall equilibrium. Nevertheless it would have been impossible to be ignorant of the fact that there existed between my parents something akin to an armed truce which resulted in a semi-permanent feeling of wariness in their children.

When letters arrived from what were clearly faraway places my mother's attention would stray from me and my narrow pre-school world and I knew that the man whose photograph hung next to the wireless had now taken her entire attention. His writing on the flimsy airmail forms was instantly recognizable and she would hold each one in both hands and a little gingerly when it arrived under the front door, staring down at it for a long time before carefully and slowly slicing the sides with a small ivory handled kitchen knife. Then it would be read and read again throughout the day and she would more than likely cry which made me tense and anxious. The airmail letter days were those when she would be likely to sing Yours a great deal and Mrs Bassant next door would ask to hear it again because she sang like an angel. *Yours til the stars lose their glory, yours til the birds cease to sing, yours to the end of life's story...* But then again when you are three or four years old you don't pay too much attention to the words that accompany popular melodies.

It was to be many years before I really understood that my father had been very much a second best choice as a husband and only accepted because he was preferable to being left On The Shelf. Every time she sang Vera Lynn's 1941 hit song in all likelihood she was dedicating each rendition to her much mourned fiancé who had died of TB in 1934. Each of the birthday cards he had given her were secreted away in the shoe box at the bottom of her wardrobe along with Very Important Papers such as our birth certificates and her marriage certificate. From time to time during those wartime years, when the house was quiet she removed the cards reverently from their tissue paper and held them gently, tenderly as if afraid they might disintegrate. One day, much later after I had learned to read I took them out myself hardly daring to breathe as I read the message and studied his grown-up writing, so different from Bernard Joseph Hendy's, less positive and defined.... *To my sweetheart on her birthday.* And when I was old enough to consider such matters I wondered what he had been like, this man who should by rights have been my father and for whom she had so often sung sad songs. And what would I be like if the dreaded TB had not claimed him? Would I be a lot better at maths perhaps? Would I have a completely different name? Would I still feel like me? And when my brother was born would he in fact turn out to be a sister instead?

Once I asked my older cousin Margaret if she had known Poor Fred but she said she didn't remember him and thought she must have been still a baby when he died. All she knew was that the aunts were fearful that my mother would never get over the loss of him and that the enormity of her grief had been great. So it had been a day of some rejoicing when Uncle Bern came along intent upon sweeping her off her feet although they had their doubts initially and our grandmother had said that some of his ideas made him sound as Thick as Pig Shit. Though for all that at the great age of fifteen Margaret thought it was better to marry somebody with daft ideas than not marry at all because nobody wanted to be an old maid.

Of course these were things destined to be discussed only rarely between my mother and her sisters because back then working class women had an enormous capacity for absorbing the good with the bad and life was simply the way it was whether you liked it or not. Better not to dwell on it unduly, simpler by far to just get on with it and *Count Your Blessings*, maybe even *Wish Upon A Star* if you became too disheartened with your lot – and naturally enough those were also melodies to be featured among family favourites.

Just getting on with it was sound advice for all who grew to adulthood in the first half of the twentieth century and followed assiduously by the man destined to become my father undoubtedly borne out of his formative years growing up in a Chatham orphanage. Our mother had invariably sniffed disapprovingly when the matter of our father's peremptory depositing into the care of the

Medway Cottage Homes was raised. Such a thing would never have happened in the Constant family where somehow or other, hard though it might be, familial care would have been taken of the poor little mite.

Surprisingly my father was always able to find an upside to orphanage living and told us it had given him a good start in life and the life was much the same as that in the British Army where he made excellent progress and earned promotions. And whilst my mother was singing her heart out in York Road, Northfleet, he got the most he could from a musical point of view out of Italy, learning a number of arias from the works of Verdi. He sang them to her when he came home on leave, explaining the tragic stories behind each one. He said he would take her to a real performance after the war, perhaps at Covent Garden where they might even see the great Beniamino Gigli himself who he explained was a bit like Richard Tauber. When she discussed this idea with her sisters they turned out to be lukewarm on the plan and Maud said you never knew where that kind of activity was going to end did you? In the end it didn't happen.

What did happen was that at the conclusion of his last period of leave and in a gesture of goodwill towards his emotionally confused wife my father surprised her with a rendering of *We'll Meet Again* whilst carrying me on his shoulders to the top of the garden. Later that evening he sang it again at The Prince Albert in Shepherd Street preceded by *E Lucevan le Stella* from Puccini's opera Tosca which my mother was surprised to find earned him enthusiastic applause. Old Mr and Mrs Bassant sitting in the Snug over their Saturday night halves of mild and bitter said you could have heard a pin drop before the clapping began because there was no doubt at all that all manner of folks were drawn to all kinds of music and that was a fact.

Many long years later during a discussion about 1940s privations with her grandson gathering information for a school project my mother commented that back in those dark wartime days there was no underestimating the mettle of the likes of Vera Lynn. Black outs and ration books were all very well of course but you could never overlook those who could stand up in front of any number of people day in and day out to sing. A gift like that she said, brought a lot of joy into people's lives and there was no doubt that's exactly what you needed to keep you going in wartime, bluebirds or no bluebirds. She had often thought, she added, that her Bern had just a little of that same kind of gift.

Never on the Never-Never

I grew up with the firm knowledge that acquiring too many things on Tick was undesirable at best, particularly when the items were those that might appear on a regular weekly shopping list. So generally we paid up front for our sugar, flour, bread and potatoes or else as my mother firmly stated – we went without! We did not go without all that often because we were also a family that prided itself on good management and those things we did go without were, I was told, those we didn't need in the first place. Mostly this revolved around her opinion and not mine or my brother's because we were rarely consulted and whilst my father was still alive neither was he.

On the other hand many of our neighbours and certainly members of our own extended family were believed to be always up to their eyeballs in debt and it was made very clear to me that this was not a good way to run your life and very nearly tantamount to digging yourself into an early grave. However even at an early age I fully understood that it was unlikely that you could become up to your eyeballs because of an overdeveloped leaning towards grocery items. It seemed clear that it was portable radios and Raleigh 3-speed bicycles that might prove to be your undoing and we most definitely did not go in for such extravagances, desirable though they might be. For one thing our 1935 Art Deco style wireless still worked perfectly well even though it was rather too awkward in size and shape to carry around with you and although I had been promised a bicycle if I worked hard and passed the 11-plus exam, when I failed the idea was not further mentioned.

My mother was proud of the fact that unlike many of our neighbours we never had to hide from the Tally Man but it was some time before I understood why he was so unpopular since his outward appearance was essentially smart and he seemed to be polite and smile a lot. He also had an appealing range of goods inside his blue van so the often prevailing attitude to him seemed curious. It was obvious even to an eight-year-old that his position hovering always between approval and animosity must have made his job unnecessarily stressful. It can't have been easy to be a York Road regular destined to knock on doors that were so often not opened, although I was aware that this also happened from time to time to the rent collector from Porter, Putt & Fletcher. Because we were Good Managers we never found ourselves in that position either and I was frequently reminded that we weren't like some scrambling to hide away on the stairs of a Monday morning on account of the rent man. These persistent warnings with regard to what could happen if you slipped from the straight and narrow fiscally had the desired effect and even now I am nervous even contemplating the use of my credit card.

From early in the twentieth century many working class families, together with those aspiring to the lower middle class, were attracted by the hire purchase schemes offered for seamless acquisition of high priced household goods that would normally be beyond their reach. However over time many of the lenders were said to abuse their positions. They were alleged to charge excessive rates, set harsh terms for repayment that frequently enabled them to reclaim goods without notice and add undue levels of interest on payments. This was finally addressed by the Hire Purchase Act of 1938, proposed by Ellen Wilkinson who was later to become Minister of Education in Clement Atlee's government. Among other things the Act restricted lenders from entering a purchaser's property without notice and it required them to clearly state the terms of all agreements. Ellen had been born into a poor but ambitious family; her father was a cotton worker who finally bettered himself by becoming an insurance agent. She had embraced socialism at an early age and eventually, inspired by the Russian Revolution of 1917, joined the British Communist Party. She was to remain a fervent lifelong supporter of better opportunities for working class girls and was largely responsible for the drive to increase the school leaving age from 14 to 15.

It became perfectly acceptable for us to start buying items of clothing from Littlewoods Mail Order Catalogue by 1947 which presumably was because one of my aunts became an Agent. The original company began in 1923 and provided venues for sports betting called Littlewoods Pools in partnership with John Moores who withdrew from the venture early on following a significant business loss in the first season. Notwithstanding these start-up hiccups, football enthusiasts like Uncle Harold became devotees immediately and generally remained so for life. And furthermore the developing business off-shoots of the game made women like my mother feel that On Tick catalogue shopping was respectable.

Littlewoods dominated some households. It seemed to me that the complete silence that was required for my tetchy uncle to fill in his weekly Pools form always coincided with our regular visit and it took an interminable amount of time during which Aunt Mag hovered over any of us under the age of twelve hissing loudly with forefinger poised on lips that we should be quiet because Uncle's Doing His Pools! And if we did not immediately pay heed she might add threateningly that he would not be best pleased if he couldn't concentrate because there was a lot at stake. This made the outcome sound like something close to a matter of life as normal continuing or being thrown out onto the streets. As for the form filler himself any intrusion into the total quiet that he demanded gave rise to a salvo of expletives of the kind only usually heard from our grandmother. His youngest daughter Ann said I was lucky that my own father was not a football follower and that she hated the Pools almost as much as going to church and the library. Knowing that she did not seem to be overly engaged in either of those activities I was suitably impressed.

The regular broadcast that so engrossed men of similar ilk could be heard weekly on the BBC and the reading of the Results was heralded by an instantly recognizable march by Hubert Bath called *Out of the Blue*. The game results themselves were read by someone called James Alexander Gordon and eventually his voice became as soporific to me as he who read the iconic Shipping Forecast. I was totally uninterested in football and as this was long before we had a television set I had never seen a game. Football was simply something that preoccupied boys until they eventually reached the age of reason and a great many of their fathers who never seemed to grow out of the habit. In those days it would have been a very odd girl indeed who expressed an interest in such an activity. Nevertheless there was something almost reassuringly hypnotic about the rhythmic voices emanating from the radio and informing listeners of the most recent successes and failures of clubs throughout the country –and like it or not I became totally familiar with their names; Aston Villa, Arsenal, Blackpool, Birmingham City, Burnley, Colchester, Everton, Huddersfield, Sheffield United, Stoke City, Tottenham Hotspur and Wolverhampton Wanderers among them. And the latter would always cause a nod or a headshake from my passionately absorbed Uncle depending upon how well that team had performed simply because Wolverhampton was his place of birth and was according to him the finest place in Britain. He said this so often that even when I was seven I wondered why he had torn himself away from the place to live in Crayford.

My younger brother was never interested in any aspect of the game even when some devious encouragers began to iron out its reputation calling it soccer and pretending it was more significant than it really was. The only attention he ever showed was brief and to Tottenham Hotspurs when he wondered why a cockerel appeared on the club's badge. Nobody knew but a long time later he discovered that they got their name from Harry Hotspur, a medieval English nobleman who appeared in Henry IV Part 1 and was noted for his riding spurs and interest in fighting cocks. Bernard's interest was transitory to say the least though he managed to note that a Turkish side also had a cockerel on their club badge and were called the Roosters whilst Bradford City were known as the Bantams whose badge was presumably similar. This was merely a quiver of curiosity towards a flurry of feathers.

Meanwhile Uncle Harold, not in the slightest bit concerned with any variety of cockerels fighting or otherwise, duly completed the Pools for years without a significant win and only gave it up when BBC TV began broadcasting the results on *Grandstand* each week. I don't remember him winning any amount that caused the slightest ripple of excitement in the family unless of course he chose not to share such an electrifying piece of news. Aunt Martha thought that was perfectly possible because Harold could be a devious piece of work if ever there was one and even his Mag had been heard to say that herself but Aunt Rose visiting from Peterborough thought he had far too big a mouth to keep it shut under such circumstances. My mother carried on knitting and wisely said nothing though later she commented that there was plenty she could have added had she been one to gossip, which of course she was not.

The Constant women were definitely more concerned with the mail order catalogue that Littlewoods first sent out to their then existing pools subscriber base in the early nineteen thirties than the game itself. The new venture had gone down well with many Pools Wives then effectively becoming retail agents, collecting money for goods ordered by friends and family. Because Aunt Maud was to eventually proudly describe herself as a Littlewoods Agent, my mother adjusted to this particular category of on Tick buying quite effortlessly. She did, however, object to the undue pressure that reared up from time to time to make more purchases than she was altogether comfortable with. And she was largely only truly at ease with pale pink or blue underclothes and nightwear in plain old fashioned fabrics like winceyette or flannel. Regardless of this though Littlewoods grew as both a retail and betting organisation and, at its height, had over 25,000 employees.

As time went by and we became a one-parent family, money became tighter than ever. A tentative exploration was made of what the Rainbow Stores in Stone Street, Gravesend could offer on what was known as the Never-Never. My mother always behaved as if she was letting the side down when she embarked upon one of these purchases, outlining all the reasons for and against the idea for several weeks in advance and generally behaving as if she was in danger of being incarcerated within a Dickensian debtors' prison. I remember her excitement when finally a much vaunted portable radio set appeared triumphantly on the front room sideboard along with the sherry trifle made in advance for Sunday's tea. Although called a sherry trifle it had simply been exposed to sherry essence and the radio beside it, maroon rexin-covered was, like its Art Deco predecessor, rather on the ungainly side to be truly classed as portable. It was explained to me that it could be plugged into a power source of course but it also worked via batteries which in fact turned out to be a very expensive way of listening to Radio Luxembourg's *Top Twenty* at 11pm each Sunday evening. But at least I could now listen in bed so at the age of fourteen I began to see that sometimes there might be a positive side to a reasonable degree of debt.

The Never-Never was never all that far from our lives no matter how hard we tried to exclude it. I was introduced to it in a more personal way via the mysterious and slightly exotic idea of Provident cheques when I was about to start work and needed a wardrobe suitable for starting this new phase of my life. After a lot of discussion as to whether it was a good idea we applied for one to equip me for the role of a commuting shorthand typist. A twenty pound cheque was to be paid back each week to the Provident Man – one pound each time but on twenty one occasions. The final momentous payment was the Provident Man's personal reward for providing the money in the first place – at least that's how I saw it. At the time this was viewed as an excellent way of buying clothes and the shops accepting the cheques all had a discreet information notice in the window. I rather liked the fact that the word Cheque was used, implying in my immature adolescent mind that I might actually be mistaken for someone who operated a Bank Account. My cousins June and Pat had both acquired their glamorous working outfits via the good offices of the Provident Man although Aunt Maud said later that for her June it was a waste as she'd ended up working as a kennel maid at the Crayford Dog Track. June said she'd never been keen on the Burgundy New Look coat and matching high heeled shoes in the first place but her mother wouldn't be told and apparently wanted her to look as smart as possible for her first job. Old Nan commented that although she said it herself, her third daughter Maud could be as silly as cats' lights at times and it wasn't any wonder at all that her June was much the same.

Being quite unaccustomed to buying new clothes I was desperately anxious to examine what the Gravesend fashion establishments had on offer and perhaps to talk loudly about Cheques as I did so and of course twenty pounds seemed like a fortune to me. We started in New Road and progressed slowly into the High Street. After several hours of vacillation I became the owner of a grey woollen Swagger style coat with a faux leopard skin collar together with an oatmeal tweed long sleeved dress, a black slim-line skirt, a red twinset and black Cuban heeled shoes with matching plastic that looked just-like-leather, shoulder bag. Quite a lot could be done with twenty pounds in May 1956. Being completely unfamiliar with the idea of owning so many new items of clothing all at once I felt distinctly light headed for several hours afterwards as I reverently examined them spread out across my bed. I was already more than a little anxious about the repayments and wondered what happened if you failed to make a payment. Did the Provident Man demand the dress back perhaps? And would he eventually return it if and when the debt was paid?

The most momentous on On-Tick, Never-Never decision was when we headed back to the Rainbow Stores in mid-1956 to seriously investigate the idea of finally becoming owners of a TV set. We were definitely the very last York Road residents to take the plunge towards the delights of the Telly and my brother said that at school he was looked at incredulously when he admitted our disadvantaged state. How could a respectable ten-year-old live without *Crackerjack*? Now, however, with my new status as a working woman earning the huge sum of five pounds per week, it was clear that we would at last be able to justify the regular twenty-five shillings weekly repayment which seemed to go on for ever. We studied a great many models and I can no longer remember whether we finally decided upon the Decca, Pye or Bush version but I do know that ours featured a smart dark French polished cabinet on slim legs and an extraordinarily impressive twelve inch screen. We ended up quite dizzy with elation that Saturday afternoon and had to revive ourselves with cups of tea from the stall in the market before heading home. Things were definitely looking up!

The set arrived on the following Tuesday and Bernard told me he had sat in school all day oblivious to everything around him, gazing through the classroom windows and imagining he could just decipher the words on vans navigating the area. Which one might be from the Rainbow Stores? He had never felt such sublime exhilaration. By the end of that week we were a trio that had feasted upon *Gunsmoke, Hancock's Half Hour, Opportunity Knocks, Sunday Night at the London Palladium* and *Armchair Theatre* to mention just a few of the entertainment gems on offer. My mother quickly decided that she loved *Dixon of Dock Green* above anything else whilst Bernard rapidly became addicted to *Zoo Quest* and was from then on a lifelong fan of David Attenborough. Owning our very own black and white television set with its vast fourteen inch screen was a critical moment in his short life and meant that he would no longer endure regular spikes of envy and resentment when local mothers called their offspring in from their regular after school play on the street to watch *Popeye* or *Worzel Gummidge*. And in those early days he even rushed home from school to take in the adventures of *Muffin the Mule* and *Andy Pandy* though he was clearly a little too old to be truly interested. Furthermore having felt seriously side-lined in June 1953 at the time of the Coronation he felt that should Queen Elizabeth ever feel the urge to repeat the grand event he would be able to watch it from the moderate comfort of his own home rather than wait hopefully to be called inside that of a neighbour. Regardless of the many arguments against as far as my brother was concerned there was undeniably a permanent place for the Never-Never in the life of a working class boy.

As for investing money in the Pools well that was a completely different matter. Old Nan always said that you didn't have a dog's chance of winning with Littlewoods because everybody knew it was rigged. For one thing you never met anyone who'd had a win did you? Not a proper win that would buy you a stand-alone house on Blackheath or even a semi-detached in Bexley. Even Mag's Harold thought he might have been better off ditching Littlewoods and throwing his lot in with Vernons. When I asked nobody seemed to know if Vernons had a catalogue of course but it's more than likely that they did.

A Bird In The Hand

It would definitely be true to say that education was not high on the priority list of my maternal grandparents. The lack of interest from certain corners of the Constants I have often somewhat flippantly documented and that frivolous attitude is in itself more than likely due to a fascination with the notion that anyone could care so little for that particular convention. However, as my brother was invariably at pains to point out, at the stage when our maternal grandmother should have been preparing her young daughters for regular school attendance the Act itself was still seen as a novel idea by a great many of the working class. Nevertheless, by the time the attention of the populace was fully occupied with the Home Front intricacies of the Great War it would be fair to say that the older Constants were at least nominally enrolled in the closest Roman Catholic School and at times when not needed for field work actually attended.

My mother in later years was fond of relating a number of nightmare experiences she had during her school days largely involving the merciless brutality of various teaching nuns. It's difficult to know how much exaggeration was involved but even if the tales were merely half true they indicate a level of cruelty that would be quite unacceptable today. According to her accounts she was caned for being absent from Sunday Mass, caned again for wearing grubby pinafores on Monday mornings and yet again for not reliably eating fish on Fridays. At seven and eight years of age she was not responsible for the family wash and definitely not put in charge of food shopping so she quite rightly felt that at times the punishments were uncalled for. She was particularly outraged by being addressed as Helen when her name was Nellie, her mother being unaware that this was a diminutive rather than a given name in the proper sense. When she tried to explain she was told she was being impertinent so she seethed with indignation instead. It's more than likely of course that the ongoing persecutions had more to do with the fact that the entire Constant family was a thorn in the side of both School and Church rather than the particular wrongdoing of one of its small members. Whatever the reason, the catalogue of misdemeanours was endless and the penalties over a number of years were severe. Quite the worst of which in her opinion was that occasioned by the dying baby thrush.

She had a habit of regularly telling us that we must never ever hold a baby bird in our hands no matter how tempting that might be should we come across one that had fallen from the nest. The heat of our hands would undoubtedly kill it we were advised and that would lead not only to a great many tears but perhaps punishment as well and nobody wanted that. Having gained our full attention she related the details of an incident concerning a particular baby bird stumbled upon on her way to school one Monday morning in her grubby pinafore already worrying because she was late. And she was late because she had been the one called upon to help her mother with the newest baby born just a few days previously. How she foolishly stopped to examine the bird, wondering if there might be any way of returning it to its rightful place, how she unwisely picked it up and decided to take it with her, carefully sheltering it from wind and rain and running in triumph towards the ultimate good sense and perception of Sister Joseph. What a good, kind, pupil that greatly feared pedagogue would then see standing before her.

But by the time she arrived the week's spelling list was starting – Piece, Niece, Achieve ... 'i before e except after c' and the woman's startled short, sharp scream as she dropped the forlorn little bundle of feathers on the desk in front of her rang in my mother's ears for many a long year. The sad little bird had already died, its demise coming about she was told on account of the hot and clumsy hands of a cruel eight-year-old. Slaughtered by the most disobedient and unruly student in the school, one who was known to regularly miss Sunday Mass and who ate meat rather than fish regardless of the day of the week. Now standing there in a pinafore that had not been washed for days she found herself responsible for the death of one of God's creatures, slain in an untimely manner by the heat of her own callous hands. She was given three strokes of the cane on each of those iniquitous hands for their wickedness. When she tearfully related the story to her mother later that day she was advised she should have known better and that the punishment must have been deserved because the Blessed Sisters surely knew best. The baby thrush, however, proved hard to forget.

It was a fact that unhappily not one of the Constant children of Maxim Road Crayford was able to take full advantage of the opportunities afforded by the new-fangled Education Act because their attendance was generally an ad hoc affair and their mother's uninterest, tinged with fear, only compounded the problem. They were not totally unintelligent children and Nellie always claimed that she was glad she learned to read, she enjoyed reading and did her very best to be present on Wednesday and Friday afternoons when there were Silent Reading periods. Perhaps even more surprisingly she revealed on more than one occasion a love of poetry, demonstrating that she still recalled verse after verse of *The Forsaken Merman* and *Home Thoughts from Abroad* though she was unsure as to the authorship of either. This predilection for the written word did little to protect her however from the school's worst excesses of minor tortures and torments and she claimed that on Monday mornings when Father Carrol's housekeeper needed help from the older girls in order to complete her duties Nellie Constant was invariably the one nominated to empty his chamber pot. Never finding it unused overnight she had to lift it carefully and negotiate the steep stairs to the floor below setting it down again in the kitchen with anxiety before opening the heavy door to the backyard where the evil looking contents could be finally emptied into the outside privy. Heaven forbid that there should there be any spills on the journey. Even Old Nan was to some extent affronted that one of her brood was so regularly selected to be responsible for the Reverend Father's overnight receptacle and said the housekeeper was a lazy trollop. She was never slighted enough though to open a debate with the woman because after all somebody had to get the job done because it would never do for the Reverend Father to find it unemptied beneath his bed as he knelt to pray the following night would it? Nellie should take a leaf out of Mag's book and that was a fact!

Mag was always described as crafty, managing to dodge not only the most unpleasant duties such as those concerning the Piss Pot of the parish priest but also a lot of the other troubles at school that so often beset Nellie. It does seem that there were times when my mother went out of her way to court disaster and that there was a part of her that half enjoyed the attention gained by becoming the family whipping boy. At the same time, however, a growing abhorrence was inculcated within her for the Roman Catholic Church which eventually led to a firm determination to keep away from it as far as possible in the future. Wisely she did not share this stance widely within the family, taking part in the rites and occasions necessitated by births, deaths and marriages over the years without undue comment except on occasion to Mag. None of them had emerged as having more than the most basic interest in religion that was necessary to still feel they had a stake in it, a right to identify themselves as part of it. All new babies were baptised in the first few months of life without incident and each went on to attend the nearest Roman Catholic school where luckily the new breed of teaching nuns proved to be less bitter and spiteful than their predecessors. By the 1930s it was not deemed quite as necessary for whole families to attend Sunday Mass on a regular basis. Good Catholic mothers after all were needed at home to prepare the roast lamb or beef, the various vegetables, the stewed fruit and custard and so for them once a month seemed to suffice to hold on to their rightful place in Catholicism as long as they went regularly to Confession. Children were just a little less likely to be cross examined about what they ate on Fridays and luckily the starched white pinafores of the Edwardian era had completely vanished.

It became relatively easy for Nellie to manage a reasonable silence over most matters pertaining to Faith even when her adored fiancé Poor Fred succumbed to TB and his family turned out to be Anglican; so peace and harmony could be maintained all round. That was a blessing because it was most unwise to deviate too widely from the opinions of the Constants. In fact a year or two after Fred's death she even told them she'd had no knowledge of where his family worshipped and it was something never broached for discussion. That was of course quite untrue but because her anguish and despair had been palpable they asked no further questions and instead they said she had suffered a Breakdown and diligently continued to feed her the pills the doctor prescribed. So she settled into her sister Mag's household almost comfortably, content to care for the children, prepare the food and do the cleaning whilst Mag worked shifts down at Vickers. Even in the 1930s Vickers-Armstrong was an organisation that distinguished itself with its forward thinking attitude towards the employment of married women. They were of course on a pay scale considerably lower than the men but this was a time when women were quite accepting of discrimination. Feminism was well into the future except for a few of the fashionable middle class. Female liberation had yet to emerge and men had families to support. As for Mag, she was delighted to become a working woman and her Harold was more than proud of her.

As the more complex details of their mother's life emerged it never became completely clear to Nellie's future children why it was she had agreed to the ill-fated marriage proposal that resulted in their birth. If those pre-wartime conversations could have been recalled it would have been as Mag said herself, as clear as daylight that she would soon need that back bedroom for her growing family. It wasn't really right that little Margaret still slept in the same room as the two boys and they were of course now quite old enough to keep an eye on her and each other. These arguments might have sounded quite specious. The Constants as they grew up had slept where and how they could, huddled together under tarpaulins during the spring and summer, so having a roof of any kind overhead was seen as a bonus, separating boys from girls an extravagance. The idea of any of them needing constant adult supervision once they could walk and talk would have caused merriment.

Nellie's future husband had revealed himself to be a Good Catholic and he had clearly been lulled into a false sense of security by the outward signs of similar commitment within the Iron Mill Lane homes he had visited. On Old Nan's kitchen wall the Bleeding Heart of Jesus was flamboyantly displayed and elsewhere among the sisters little statuettes of the Virgin clothed in blue, some holding the infant Jesus in their arms sat on sideboards. The plethora of small children had familiar names that served to seal his overall approval. He was not to know that he was making an error of judgement, neither had he at that stage been told the story of the baby thrush that had died in overheated hands in 1916.

Appreciating the Cottage Homes

Although there is no record of the actual level of interest in education my paternal grandparents might have had, in the long run it mattered little because my father was fortunate enough to have been received into the Chatham Workhouse at a tender age along with his baby sister. This wasn't nearly as bad as it might sound and in fact it was not by any means his first experience of the place. Strictly speaking the term Workhouse had for several years been replaced by Poor Law Institution and although those entering had previously been known as Paupers they were now referred to by the more up to date and cutting edge term Poor Persons. None of this of course was of much interest to my four-year-old father.

His mother Kate displayed an enduring level of neglect that totally eclipsed the worst excesses of Old Nan Constant, her mothering being liberally peppered with police charges, prison sentences and accusations of prostitution. Her husband Charles had abandoned her because the two youngest of their eight children having been conceived whilst he was away at sea were unlikely to be his. The rest of his family, all living in the Medway area, were supportive of this stance. By the time Kate came before the Stipendiary Magistrate at Chatham Police Court in November 1913 her mistreatment of the two children remaining in her care was described as the worst case of neglect the NSPCC had seen in a very long time.

So shocking were the details they were widely reported in local newspapers and the children swiftly removed to the safety of what all the locals still called The Workhouse. Their mother was sentenced to six months hard labour. This turned out to be a very good outcome for Bernard Joseph who ended up in the long term care of the Medway Cottage Homes and was not to see his mother again for more than thirty years. Unfortunately all contact with his baby sister, Elizabeth Mary was also severed and it is not known what became of her although she may well have been adopted. Although when she learned of his history my mother was appalled by the fact that he had ended up in institutional care, my father always considered it had been a stabilising influence in his life and very quickly came to believe that from an educational viewpoint Nellie and her sisters had been dealt a much worse hand overall.

The Cottage Homes in Pattens Lane, Chatham had been purpose built in the latter part of the nineteenth century as a small self-contained village in which seriously disadvantaged children lived in groups of ten to twenty each with a house mother, boys separately from girls. They had their own school on site together with a chapel, sports facilities and training workshops for metalwork and carpentry. All pupils learned to swim, there was opportunity to learn to play musical instruments and from time to time there were outings to Broadstairs and Southend funded by local church groups. It is unlikely that any of these opportunities would have ever been forthcoming under the chaotic maternal care of Kate Hendy.

Warm clothing and sturdy boots were provided along with an adequate supply of food which was generally plain except at Christmas. As they grew older obliging and hungry lads like Bernard Joseph Hendy volunteered as scullery assistants which meant that from time to time an extra bread and jam or pudding ration might be purloined. Any kitchen-related duties would invariably afford the young worker such perks as sole charge of stale bread discarded from the Friday bread pudding making. This task came with instructions to break it into suitably sized pieces to be managed by the four, five and six year olds who were to distribute it to the evening gathering of squabbling pigeons. Not all of the bread reached the birds of course and the untidy assembly grew more raucous and clamorous by the minute as it disappeared into the mouths of the youngest boys. Bernard Joseph enjoyed the shiver of munificence as he walked among them ensuring that each child had a portion of stale bread for dissemination. This was his quasi-family, these small children pseudo-siblings. He enjoyed his role as a virtual big brother and he quite liked his house mother.

Discipline at the Cottage Homes was definitely firm but if you kept your head down, as all sensible lads resolved to do, its worst excesses could be avoided. It was not wise to allow yourself to become a bed wetter or to draw undue attention with smart remarks that made other boys laugh because then you surely would find life could be unpleasant. It was also a good idea to pay attention to school work and offer to tidy classrooms. A helpful attitude meant you were invariably one of those allowed first choice of reading books and might even result in your name coming to the top of the list for visits to museums or to the Pantomime. Quite apart from that good behaviour earned you much coveted proper swimming lessons and meant that the small but regular fortnightly pocket money allowance was never reduced by fines that so plagued the miscreants. Life was by no means unpleasant for a boy who kept his wits about him and had learned to get by without a surfeit of parental love and affection in his life.

In fact the austere and disciplined learning environment with its over-abundance of books by Charles Dickens and classroom walls covered with maps of the world suited my father admirably. He never tired of examining those fortunate areas of the known world operating within the confines of the Great British Empire and he vowed that in the mysterious future he would travel widely. Over the years within the relative comfort of these predictable environs he learned rapidly and with ease, was always top in Mental Arithmetic, rarely made spelling mistakes and usually had his socks pulled up to his knees and his boots polished to perfection. For just over a decade he did not rub shoulders much with outside children, those described as Ordinary with mothers and fathers and real siblings, neither did he appear to have any memory whatsoever of any of his birth family. For him they were good years.

He had got on as a Cottage Homes boy very well overall but nonetheless something happened to rupture this equanimity when he was thirteen or fourteen years old because it was then he damaged his unblemished record of excellent behaviour and ran away vowing never to return. Unfortunately he chose not to share the details of this most exciting story with me and if he did so with my mother she chose likewise. He set off apparently after lights out with a bread roll wrapped in a handkerchief and two shillings of laboriously saved pocket money. This was revealed to me by my brother after a great deal of genealogical research in more recent years and may or may not have been completely accurate. His aim had been to reach London and find a job, preferably as a motor cycle mechanic which was something he knew little about but was exceedingly keen to learn. How he made his way to the outer reaches of North London to a modest mock Tudor estate is not known but somehow or other he did. An over-excited ten-year-old boy called Stephen Woodman, the only child and son of a ledger clerk, hid him in the garden shed at 29 Methuen Road, Edgware just beyond the neat rows of climbing beans for almost a week. He supplied him with food stolen from his unknowingly generous mother's pantry and desperately wanted to join him on the next part of the adventure, promising to steal him a map of the area with perhaps clear indication of the way to Wales. It was whilst searching through his father's possessions in near darkness late at night for such a map that he was discovered and unable to control his excitement any longer blurted out to his startled parents that there was a runaway boy in the shed.

And so it was that my father was returned to Chatham quite quickly to the disappointment of both boys. Young Stephen, greatly impressed by Bernard Joseph's resolution and mettle, stayed in touch with him for years afterwards, sending regular letters to the Cottage Homes and was eventually to be known to me and my brother as Uncle Steve. It wasn't until after the death of my father that he revealed the story of how their relationship began.

When Bernard Joseph reached the obligatory age for leaving the care of the Homes a job was found for him at the cement works in Northfleet together with a relative to lodge with, traced apparently without undue problem. The first two weeks of his Board was to be financed by one of the funds established for the purpose. His older brother Walter Francis Hendy, now married and living at 119 Waterdales, was deemed a suitable landlord and my father moved in without delay sharing a room with several teenage nephews. It was then that he began to save for a motorbike and reclaim his heritage by embracing Catholicism.

The details of his progress through life over the next thirteen or fourteen years are unknown but on a Saturday evening in early 1939 he was taken by a group of motor cycle enthusiasts to The Jolly Farmers in Crayford where he met my mother and two of her sisters. By that time he was the proud owner of an Ariel Red Hunter cycle that boasted only one previous very careful owner. He was also a regular Sunday Mass attendee at St John the Evangelist Church in Gravesend. He was undeniably anxious at the age of twenty-nine to settle down and create a family of his own. Nellie Constant, unmarried, demure and associated with the Right Church seemed ideal and in any case it was about time he was getting on with it.

Urged on by her sisters who all agreed marriage would be good for her and she was lucky to be asked at the great age of thirty-one, my mother did not hesitate for long although she did have doubts. The main obstacle as far as she was concerned was that he wasn't a patch on her Fred but Mag said she was bound to think that but she shouldn't let it stand in the way of good sense. Her Fred would have wanted her to find somebody else after all these years and it could even be that he was looking down and had directed Bern her way. Nellie didn't entirely agree with this considering it a fanciful notion but she didn't argue too much either because when all was said and done he did seem a nice enough chap and nobody could accuse him of being a drinker for instance. A single pint once a week or perhaps two if really pushed was quite enough for him, nothing like Mag's Harold or Maud's George who both drank like fish. He didn't use bad language either and if you only heard the language used by some that she didn't care to name it would make your hair curl, it really would. So to be fair she could do a lot worse.

So her brother Edgar booked an available space with the priest at St Mary of the Crays for Monday 7th August at 11am, he and two Constant sisters agreeing to be witnesses. The fourth witness was a cousin from the Hendy side called Arthur May. My mother wore a cream satin dress and carried a spray of orange blossom and everybody said she looked a picture. Four of her sisters were bridesmaids in pale blue satin, Rose, Phyllis, Violet and Freda. She hadn't really wanted to have Freda if the truth be known but Old Nan was adamant and Mag said don't upset the apple cart, it never pays. Mag's little Margaret was the flower girl and Maud's Desmond was the page boy, both in cream with blue sashes and looking as if butter wouldn't melt. To be fair little Margaret was always a well behaved child but Maud spoilt her kids rotten and Desmond could be a real tartar at times and if he was hers he would get what he deserved and that was a fact. That day, however, he was as good as gold. She had to admit it, she'd definitely enjoyed the ceremony and the fuss involved in the taking of photos and the wedding breakfast in the hall had been a real treat, everybody said so. It had been a most agreeable day though not the happiest in her life because that had been the day she and Poor Fred got engaged but nevertheless a good day. Everything had gone well all things considered and it was only the future that really concerned her.

At some stage in those early days of marriage she took courage and discussed with her new husband topics that perhaps she should have raised earlier. The most significant by far were her grave reservations regarding some aspects of Catholicism and she took pains to emphasise that she thought the teaching nuns to be particularly cruel and that she would be reluctant to release any future children into their care. A Roman Catholic wedding was one thing and was over and done with before you could say Jack Robinson and as Mag quite rightly pointed out, upsetting the apple cart would be foolish. On the other hand year after year in a religious school was quite a different matter. If that could be avoided by setting the cat among the pigeons then that was the way it had to be, apple cart or no apple cart.

How much heed my father actually paid to the revelations is completely lost but what is evident is that a great many altercations took place over the following years with regard to the Holy Catholic Church and exactly how my brother and I should be taking part in it. There would have undoubtedly been a great many more disagreements had the Second World War not intervened and deftly removed him from our lives for a number of years.

Our baptisms were problematical and the precise details of my own are a total mystery. The only aspect recalled by those present and now still living such as my cousin Margaret is that there was a last minute complete change of name announced by Nellie in unusually firm tones that brooked no argument, startling whoever was officiating and greatly embarrassing my father. My brother inexplicably was baptised at St Mark's Anglican Church in Rosherville in an obvious act of complete defiance and again there was a name change, though this time less significant. As far as the schools we were to attend were concerned there of course eventuated even more disharmony. I was deftly enrolled in St Botolph's before my father was demobbed from the army. Naturally enough he was later to retaliate and my brother was registered into St Joseph's in Springhead Road when he was still only four years old. My mother, enraged and aghast, was heard to complain to the aunts that he had done so Behind Her Back whilst she was gossiping with Grace Bennett one Friday afternoon. The only good thing about it was that it was on our doorstep and she was able to view what was going on in the playground from the garden gate. The moment one of those nuns laid a finger on her son she would be over there like greased lightning to clean them rotten.

Regular Church attendance heralded even more problems and once he returned to us my father bought me a Missal for Roman Catholic children and took me to Sunday Mass himself each week which I did not altogether enjoy. My mother sent me to the Methodist Chapel Sunday School in the afternoons which I quite liked because there were stories and orange juice and ginger biscuits and sometimes transfers to adorn hands and arms with. It would be fair to say I grew up under a surfeit of differing beliefs and learned always to be wary when discussing them. Those childhood Sundays of memory were never completely agreeable days. Even now Sunday is my least liked day of the week, the day where unpleasant pieces of the past live. Some of us have most liked days on the other hand, days that are far easier to pick from recall and examine. For my father they were probably those when he walked as a kind of older brother among his pseudo siblings supervising the casting of stale bread to gatherings of pigeons. They were good days and when in future years his new in-laws spoke in whispers about his mother, pitying him and saying he must have been a Poor Little Soul, he could only wonder at their ignorance.

You can find more reminiscences from Jean Hendy-Harris in *Chalk Pits and Cherry Stones, Eight Ten to Charing Cross, In Disgrace with Fortune, More than Just Skeletons,* and *Sunday's Child.*

Chalk Pits Press

https://jeanhendyharriswrites.blogspot.com/

Printed in Great Britain
by Amazon